Consumer Protection Handbook

Section of Antitrust Law

Defending Liberty
Pursuing Justice

This volume should be officially cited as:

ABA SECTION OF ANTITRUST LAW,
CONSUMER PROTECTION HANDBOOK (2004)

Cover design by ABA Publishing.

Library of Congress Control Number: 2004104052
ISBN: 1-59031-368-2

Discounts are available for books ordered in bulk. Special consideration is given to state bars, CLE programs, and other bar-related organizations. Inquire at Publications Planning & Marketing, American Bar Association, 750 North Lake Shore Drive, Chicago, Illinois 60611.

06 05 04 03 02   5 4 3 2 1

CONTENTS

Chapter 3 – State Consumer Protection Law and Enforcement

Appendix A – Excerpts of Important Federal, Uniform, and State Consumer Protection Statutes

Appendix B – List of State Little FTC Acts, UDAP, and General Consumer Protection Statutes

FOREWORD

The Section of Antitrust Law of the American Bar Association presents this *Consumer Protection Handbook* as an introductory guide to the principles of state and federal consumer protection law. This book represents the Section of Antitrust Law's most substantial publication to date concerned solely with the consumer protection field, and reflects the growing importance of consumer protection law to antitrust lawyers and to other practitioners, to business firms, and to the general public.

For several reasons, consumer protection law has special relevance to antitrust practitioners. The most influential single authority on consumer protection, the Federal Trade Commission, is also a prominent feature of the antitrust landscape. In recent years, there has been increasing cooperation and cross-pollination between the FTC's Competition and Consumer Protection Bureaus. In addition, the statutes that govern antitrust and consumer protection are intertwined – not only the FTC Act, but the numerous state laws that combine "unfair competition" claims (often cognizable as antitrust violations) with unfair and deceptive acts and practices. It's hardly surprising, then, that complaints by aggrieved competitors often allege both antitrust and consumer protection causes of action.

This handbook also contains much of value for the non-antitrust attorney. It has been designed to fill the need for a concise, basic summary of consumer protection principles for the general practitioner and corporate counsel. Especially with the advent of e-commerce, firms are potentially subject to more different consumer protection laws, in more jurisdictions, than ever before. The *Consumer Protection Handbook* is not the beginning and end of research on these laws, but it should be uniquely useful as a general orientation and as a starting point for in-depth research when the need arises.

We are deeply grateful to the Consumer Protection Committee of the section and the many attorneys who committed substantial time and effort to this handbook. Special thanks are due to Robert M. Langer and John E. Villafranco, the immediate past and present chairs of the committee, for their inspiration and editorial stewardship on this handbook, and to August T. Horvath, a vice chair, for the drafting and revisions.

February 2004

Kevin E. Grady
Chair, Section of Antitrust Law
American Bar Association
2003-2004

PREFACE

The purpose of this handbook is to provide legal practitioners who are nonspecialists in consumer protection law with a concise guide to its basic principles. The emphasis is on the law as it pertains to false advertising, unfair and deceptive trade practices, and privacy. There are many more statutes affecting consumer welfare than can even be mentioned in a treatment of this kind. This guide provides the general principles of the most important consumer protection laws, an overview of the avenues available to the potential complainant and the risks faced by a potential defendant, and a starting point for further research.

The handbook opens with a discussion of the fundamental issues in consumer protection law. The myriad laws that govern this area vary substantially, but the core consumer protection principles that run through them are consistent. Chapter 1 of this book notes major differences among the different strains of consumer protection legislation and jurisprudence, with the caveat that the practitioner must investigate the provisions of laws applicable to his or her jurisdiction. The statutes addressed in detail in this volume are Section 5 of the Federal Trade Commission (FTC) Act, which defines the unfair and deceptive practices regulated by the FTC; Section 43(a) of the Lanham Act, which creates a federal private cause of action for false and misleading advertising; and the various state consumer protection and unfair and deceptive practices (UDAP) statutes enforced by state Attorneys General, by other agencies, and by private plaintiffs.

This book also provides a brief description of the enforcement powers and available remedies, both for public and private litigants, under the major consumer protection statutes. Again, variations are alluded to where possible, but the emphasis is on the general risks faced by a violator of false advertising, unfair or deceptive trade practices, or privacy laws across most jurisdictions. Chapter 2 discusses consumer protection enforcement under federal law, both by the government – that is, the FTC – and by private plaintiffs under the Lanham Act. Strictly speaking, as discussed below, the Lanham Act is not a consumer protection law, as it creates a cause of action exclusively for competitors alleging commercial harm. But because advertising violations under the Lanham Act can be predicated on some of the same activities that give rise to violations of the FTC Act and other consumer protection laws, the

Lanham Act is akin to these laws in both its practical effect on businesses and its ultimate benefits for consumers.

Chapter 3 shifts to state law, where the mosaic of consumer protection statutes, common law principles, and enforcement organizations presents a challenge to any general treatment. State advertising laws are subject to such myriad variations that a work of this size can do no more than sketch their broadest themes. Where an issue arises in practice, close examination of the statutory and case law in the relevant jurisdiction is essential. Nonetheless, when commencing research into a possible violation, the practitioner is well served by a broad understanding of the types of practices proscribed in many of the states, and the sources from which challenges may come.

Appendix A to this volume contains the full text of the most relevant sections of the FTC Act, the Lanham Act, and representative state unfair and deceptive acts and practices (UDAP) statutes. Also provided, in Appendix B, is a list of the titles and citations of the primary UDAP statutes in all 50 states, to provide the practitioner with a starting point for further research.

A great deal of time, effort, and research went into the preparation of the *Consumer Protection Handbook*. The primary drafting responsibility was shouldered by August T. Horvath, who also undertook the process of preparing this volume for publication. Without his hard work (and good humor), there would be no handbook – plain and simple. Several individuals assisted in researching, revising, or editing portions of this handbook. James A. Wilson, the ABA Antitrust Section's Publications Officer, conceived this book and provided crucial support as liaison to the Books and Treatises Committee, without which it would never have seen publication. Robert M. Langer, who chaired the Consumer Protection Committee at the time of this handbook's inception, supplied much of the inspiration and impetus for the volume, as well as continuing input as the various drafts progressed toward publication. Helene D. Jaffe, Irving Scher, and Bruce A. Colbath, of Weil, Gotshal & Manges, provided invaluable comments and suggestions. The rest of the Consumer Protection Committee leadership – Lesley Fair, Julie Brill, and Thomas Zych – reviewed numerous drafts of this manuscript and greatly enhanced the final product. Randi W. Singer and Alison Fitzpatrick contributed research to all chapters of the handbook. Svetlana Gans provided willing and tireless assistance in getting the text and citations ready for final publication.

The *Consumer Protection Handbook* was extensively reviewed by Books and Treatises Committee members Michael H. Knight and Neil W. Imus. The ABA Antitrust Section Council reviewers were Robert M. Langer and Kevin J. O'Connor. Finally, we could not have met the deadline for publication of this handbook without the support of the staff at Weil, Gotshal & Manges.

John E. Villafranco
Chair, Consumer Protection Committee
Section of Antitrust Law
American Bar Association
2003-2004

OVERVIEW OF CONSUMER PROTECTION ISSUES

Consumer protection law is an expanding, rapidly developing, and highly visible field. All of us are consumers who can readily detect both consumer protection transgressions and the effects of consumer protection law and regulation in our daily lives. Legal practitioners must be aware that consumer protection problems, besides the direct pecuniary risks they present to firms, are among the most likely forms of misconduct to be reported in the media and potentially harm a firm's reputation with its customers.[1] Especially with the advent of the Internet, previously local or regional businesses are expanding to new markets, often where they have no physical presence, but where they may be subject to new state and local regulatory regimes. For many commercial attorneys, these factors have given consumer protection law new relevance.

By all accounts, exploiting consumers is big business. Of course, there are no official statistics documenting the size of the fraud industry. However, the cost certainly runs into many billions. In 1999, the FTC estimated the annual cost of mail fraud alone at $3 billion to $40 billion.[2] Telemarketing fraud has been estimated to cost consumers an additional $40 billion.[3] In 1996, the FTC estimated that deceptive marketing of health care products alone costs $100 billion.[4] Almost anyone with an e-mail inbox now receives deceptive appeals on a daily basis. In the post-September-11th world, even terrorist organizations are accused of raising funds through consumer protection violations such as credit card fraud.[5]

---

[1] For example, recent disclosures of passenger information by Jet Blue caused numerous news stories suggesting that the airline's image with consumers had been tarnished. *See, e.g.*, Micheline Maynard, *Jet Blue Moves to Repair Its Image after Sharing Files*, N.Y. TIMES, Sept. 23, 2003.

[2] Press Release, Fed. Trade Comm'n, *Catch the Bandit in Your Mail Box* (Oct. 5, 1999), *available at* http://www.ftc.gov/opa/1999/10/bandit3pr.htm.

[3] Montana Department of Administration Telemarketing Fraud Unit, TELEMARKETING PREVENTION BROCHURE, available at http://www.state.mt.us/doa/consumerProtection/Downloads/TelemarkPrevention.pdf.

[4] FED. TRADE COMM'N, 1996 ANNUAL REPORT, 1996 WL 910117, *available at* http://www.ftc.gov/os/ar96/.

[5] Don van Natta, Jr., *Terrorists Blaze a New Money Trail*, N.Y. TIMES, Sept. 27, 2003, at 1.

And these facts concern mainly the flagrant offenders, leaving aside the uncounted amount that consumers spend each year on products and services that do not meet their purveyors' advertising claims.

When the practitioner encounters a problem in the areas covered by this handbook, the resources contained and cited in this handbook should be a valuable first step. The best next step will depend on the nature of the problem. If the matter involves the FTC, the Commission's comprehensive website supplies extensive information on the FTC's enforcement program, procedures, and perspectives on relevant law.[6] By the same token, when dealing with a state Attorney General, that A.G.'s website – and possibly also that of the National Association for Attorneys General (NAAG)[7] – is usually of value, although there is variation in how much information of use to practitioners is provided from state to state.

Among third-party legal resources, the Commerce Clearing House (CCH) Trade Regulation Reports covers many decisions, consent orders, and policy statements that are not (or not yet) published in more conventional reporters. The Bureau of National Affairs (BNA) Antitrust & Trade Regulation Report can also be a useful source for current developments, although it does not reprint the primary documents. The National Consumer Law Center publishes an extensive, plaintiff-oriented guide to state UDAP statutes.[8] In some (though all too few) states, authoritative guides to consumer protection law within the state have been published.[9] Finally, membership in the American Bar Association Antitrust Section's Consumer Protection Committee brings with it access to an informative website, a growing base of information and expertise, access to seminars and continuing legal education programs on timely consumer protection topics, and current developments reported in the Committee's newsletter, *Consumer Protection Update*.[10]

Before considering the enforcement of consumer protection law, this chapter sets forth the basic substantive elements of the major consumer protection offenses and causes of action. The first part of this chapter discusses the law of deception, the broadest of these concepts.[11] Within deception law, one of the most extensively litigated and well developed

---

[6]   *See* http://www.ftc.gov/html.

[7]   *See* http://www.naag.org/html.

[8]   NAT'L CONSUMER LAW CENTER INC., UNFAIR AND DECEPTIVE ACTS AND PRACTICES, 5TH ED. (2001).

[9]   *See, e.g.*, ROBERT M. LANGER ET AL., CONNECTICUT UNFAIR TRADE PRACTICES, Connecticut Practice Series vol. 12 (2003).

[10]   Available at http://www.abanet.org/antitrust/committees/consumer/home.html.

[11]   *See infra* 1.A.

areas is that of false advertising, which is treated in a separate section of the chapter.[12] The other major component of consumer protection law, and a rising area of enforcement by the FTC and state agencies, is unfair trade practices, discussed in this chapter's third part.[13] Finally, privacy law, an increasingly important and high-profile field that straddles deception and unfairness, is outlined.[14]

A. DECEPTION AND CONSUMER FRAUD

"Deception" in consumer protection law is a legal concept of impressive breadth. Within the definition of deception fall transgressions that include out-and-out scams, advertising that is disseminated in good faith but is inadequately substantiated, and packaging or promotional material that is accurate but fails to comply with complex statutory labeling requirements. This section explores the broad principles running through the various forms of deception articulated by legislators and enforcement agencies, and relates them to the elements of common-law fraud that are the wellspring of deception law.

1. Deception - Traditional Definition

FTC and federal jurisprudence traditionally has defined a deceptive practice as one that (1) has a tendency or capacity to mislead (2) a substantial number of consumers (3) in a material way.[15] Most statutes governing deceptive practices incorporate, at least by implication, some variation of this definition. However, many statutes do not offer a clean definition of a deceptive practice. The Uniform Deceptive Trade Practices Act (UDTPA), the basis of several state UDAP laws, contains a twelve-part definition of deceptive practices consisting of eleven specific practices followed by the catch-all phrase, "...any other conduct which similarly creates a likelihood of confusion or of misunderstanding."[16] This phrase implies that the practice must be likely to mislead, but offers little guidance on the number and/or type of consumers that must be misled, or on the materiality of the misrepresentation (other than that it is "similar" to the enumerated categories).

---

[12]   *See infra* 1.B.

[13]   *See infra* 1.C.

[14]   *See infra* 1.D.

[15]   *See* Am. Home Prods. Corp. v. FTC, 695 F.2d 681, 686-87 (3d Cir. 1982); Sears, Roebuck & Co. v. FTC, 258 F. 307, 311 (7th Cir. 1919).

[16]   Uniform Deceptive Trade Practices Act § 2(a)(12), 7A ULA 265 (1966), *available at* http://www.law.upenn.edu/bll/ulc/ulc_frame.htm.

Notably missing from almost all definitions of a deceptive practice in consumer protection law is any element of knowledge, intent, or *scienter*.[17] The FTC and state enforcement agencies enforce their consumer protection mandate under essentially a strict liability regime. Plaintiffs in private suits under the Lanham Act and under state UDAP statutes likewise generally need not allege or prove any *mens rea* except where extraordinary damages and other punitive remedies are sought – although, occasionally, even treble damages may be awarded with no evidence of willfulness.[18] Where state UDAP statutes do appear to require some level of intent on the part of the defendant, the case law under those statutes should be scrutinized closely. Often, the required intent will be watered down in practice to, for example, the requirement that the representation being challenged was made intentionally, but not necessarily with intent to deceive.[19]

In addition, modern definitions of deceptive practices differ from traditional fraud claims in requiring no allegation or evidence that anyone was, in fact, deceived by the misrepresentation or acted on it to his or her detriment. This difference from the common law of fraud reflects the consumerist orientation of consumer protection statutes. Some courts have even identified the "fundamental purpose" of UDAP statutes as the elimination of traditional proof requirements for fraud.[20] Proof of actual harm may, however, be needed to establish damages, depending on the particular statute at issue.[21] In cases where the sole relief sought is injunctive, the most common formulation of "deception" requires only that the defendant's action have the "capacity" to deceive.[22]

But whom must the act have the capacity to deceive? This is an actively litigated question, because statutes and regulations generally are silent on the question. Some consumers certainly are more easily deceived than others. In its earlier decisions under the capacity-to-deceive standard, the FTC generally took the position that a practice is deceptive as long as it can deceive the "ignorant," the "credulous," the

---

17   *See infra* 1.B.4.

18   *See, e.g.,* Ramandham v. N.J. Mfg. Ins. Co., 455 A.2d 1134, 1135-36 (N.J. Super. App. Div. 1982); Marshall v. Miller, 302 N.C. 539, 546 (1981); Pennington v. Singleton, 606 S.W.2d 682, 690 (Tex. 1980).

19   *See, e.g.,* State *ex rel.* Corbin v. Tolleson, 773 P.2d 490, 503 (Ariz. App. 1989); Ashlock v. Sunwest Bank, N.A., 753 P.2d 346, 347 (N.M. 1988).

20   *See, e.g.,* Thomas v. Sun Furniture & Appliance Co., 399 N.E.2d 567, 569-70 (1978) (requiring proof of intent "would effectively emasculate [Ohio's UDAP law] and contradict its fundamental purpose").

21   *See infra* 3.C.1.b.

22   *See infra* 3.A.2.

"unthinking," or the least sophisticated consumer.[23] At the same time, a practice was not considered deceptive if only an insignificant and unrepresentative segment of the public would be deceived.[24] Taken together, these two standards suggest an unflattering view of the general level of consumer sophistication and intelligence.

Although, as discussed in subparagraph 2 below, the FTC in 1983 appeared to depart from the credulous-consumer standard,[25] various state enforcement authorities and both state and federal courts had by that time built up a substantial body of jurisprudence based on the concept. As a result, substantial remnants of the older standard remain.[26] The practitioner thus must be attuned to the specific standard that will be employed in his or her case.

In sum, a party can be found to have committed a deceptive practice, including false advertising, under the FTC Act, the Lanham Act, and/or most state consumer protection statutes – all discussed below in more detail – without intending to make a false representation, without knowing its representation to be false, with good faith in the truth of the claim, and without actually having deceived any particular consumer or number of consumers. This does not mean that, when the FTC or a state Attorney General is conducting an investigation or negotiating a settlement, or when a court is meting out penalties, such a party will be treated the same as a con artist who made a similarly false representation knowingly and with every intention of deceiving consumers.[27] Indeed, Government enforcement agencies and courts alike tend to reserve particular ire for willful violators.

---

[23]   *See* Charles of the Ritz Distribs. Corp. v. FTC, 143 F.2d 676, 679 (2d Cir. 1944).

[24]   *See* Heinz W. Kirchner, 63 F.T.C. 1282 (1963), *aff'd*, 337 F.2d 751 (9th Cir. 1964).

[25]   *See infra* 1.A.2.

[26]   *See, e.g.,* Good v. Broyhill Furniture, Inc., No. C041176, 2003 WL 21760027, at *11 (Cal. Ct. App. July 31, 2003) (holding a California trial court's reliance on *In re* Levitz Furniture Corp., 88 F.T.C. 263 (1976), was misplaced, in part because the narrower post-1983 standard for likelihood to mislead subsequently adopted by the FTC is now to be used in California).

[27]   *See* Warner-Lambert Co. v. FTC, 562 F.2d 749, 763 n.70 (D.C. Cir. 1977), *cert. denied*, 435 U.S. 950 (1978) (in ordering corrective advertising, declining to require "confessional" preamble, "contrary to prior advertising," because respondent's record was consistent with good faith in making prior claims); *see also infra* 3.B.

2.   *Deception – New FTC Definition*

In 1983, the FTC issued its current Policy Statement on Deception,[28] in which it adopted a revised definition of the term "deceptive." Under this new definition, to be deceptive, a representation, omission, or practice must be:

1.   likely to mislead consumers, who
2.   are presumed by the Commission to be acting reasonably in the circumstances,[29] and
3.   must be "material."[30]

As with traditional notions of fraud, the respondent's intent is not formally relevant to the modern definition. Again, however, the offender's good faith, both at the time of the alleged practice and after contact with the FTC is initiated, may impact the manner in which the Commission conducts its investigation and/or litigation.

Also still absent under the modern formulation is any requirement that actual consumers have been deceived. Under the FTC Act, a practice is unlawful merely for being *likely* to mislead consumers.[31] At the time of the FTC's Policy Statement, there were debates – including among the FTC Commissioners themselves – over whether "likely to mislead" is a different standard than having the "tendency or capacity" to mislead.[32] It could also be debated whether a "reasonable" consumer is more or less likely to be misled than a "substantial number" of consumers. The majority view within the Commission has been that the

---

[28]   Letter from James C. Miller III, FTC Chairman, to John D. Dingell, Chair of House Comm. on Energy & Commerce (Oct. 14, 1983), *reprinted in* 4 Trade Reg. Rep. (CCH) ¶ 13,205, *available at* http://www.ftc.gov/bcp/policystmt/ad-decept.htm (hereinafter, "FTC Deception Statement").

[29]   The "circumstances" include allowances for the particular group of consumers at whom the practice may be targeted, such as children.

[30]   *See* Stouffer Foods Corp., Docket No. 9250, slip op. at 3 (Sept. 26, 1994); Kraft, Inc., 114 F.T.C. 40, 120 (1991), *aff'd and enforced,* 970 F.2d 311 (7th Cir. 1992), *cert. denied,* 113 S. Ct. 1254 (1993); Removatron Int'l Corp., 111 F.T.C. 206, 308-09 (1988) (citing *e.g.,* Southwest Sunsites, Inc. v. FTC, 785 F.2d 1431, 1436 (9th Cir.), *cert. denied,* 107 S. Ct. 109 (1986)); Intl. Harvester Co., 104 F.T.C. 949, 1056 (1984); Cliffdale Assocs., Inc., 103 F.T.C. 110, 164-65 (1984); *see generally* FTC Deception Statement, *supra* note 28.

[31]   *See* FTC Deception Statement, *supra* note 28.

[32]   *See* Cliffdale Assocs., Inc., 103 F.T.C. 110, 184-85, 190 (1984) (dissenting statements of Commissioners Pertschuk and Bailey) (interpreting 1983 statement as precluding FTC from challenging practices with a mere tendency to deceive).

1983 Statement did not change the FTC's enforcement objectives, and this appears to have been borne out by the FTC's enforcement actions.[33]

Facially, the post-1983 FTC deception standard appears more restrictive than the traditional conception that any practice capable of misleading even the most credulous consumers can be deceptive. The current standard, however, makes special allowances for any targeted group of consumers that may be especially vulnerable to misleading appeals, whether by innate characteristics or by circumstances. Children, for example, are regarded as naïve, unsophisticated, and vulnerable, and advertising directed to children has been an FTC enforcement priority, under which the Commission employs a very low standard for determining whether ads are likely to deceive.[34] The FTC similarly considers whether specific advertising appeals targeted at other impressionable groups of consumers are likely to deceive members of the target group. Consumers who are temporarily more vulnerable to advertising messages because of circumstances such as the recent loss of a home, the death of a family member, or even the desire to lose weight or reverse hair loss also are accorded special protection by the flexible likely-to-deceive standard.[35] Finally, even in the case of national advertising aimed at broad audiences, the likely-to-deceive standard clearly does not imply that *most* consumers need be misled, but only a significant minority.[36] In effect, these applications build much of the old credulous-consumer standard back into the likely-to-deceive standard.

3. *Consumer Fraud*

Causes of action for fraud originate in the common law. Traditionally, common law fraud consisted of five elements: (1) a false representation, (2) the defendant's intentional making of that false representation expecting reliance, (3) defendant's knowledge of the falsity of the representation (*scienter*), (4) reliance on that false

---

[33]   *See id.* at 168-69. The Ninth Circuit, however, has held that the Policy Statement standard imposes a higher burden on the FTC than the traditional standard in showing that an act or practice is deceptive. *See Southwest Sunsites*, 785 F.2d at 1436.

[34]   *See* Ideal Toy Corp., 64 F.T.C. 297, 310 (1964); *see also* Roscoe B. Starek III, The ABCs at the FTC: Marketing and Advertising to Children, Summary of Prepared Remarks of Commissioner before the Minnesota Institute of Legal Education (July 25, 1997), *available at* http://www.ftc.gov/speeches/starek/minnfin.htm.

[35]   *See Heinz W. Kirchner*, 63 F.T.C. at 1290.

[36]   *See id.*

representation by the plaintiff, and (5) damages to the plaintiff as a result of that reliance.[37]

Compared with the deception standards described above, proving fraud often presents a stiff burden for plaintiffs. Even so, fraud continues to be alleged in many consumer protection cases. The potential payoff is that success on a fraud claim can result in the award of punitive damages in many jurisdictions. In addition, fraud is a cause of action with very broad applicability and can be used in some situations where statutory deceptive practices claims may not be available.

The Federal Trade Commission compiles statistics on consumer fraud, based on its consumer outreach and surveillance efforts. In its annual report for 2002, the FTC reported that the number of fraud complaints rose from 220,000 in 2001 to 380,000 in 2002 and that the loss to consumers relating to these complaints grew from $160 million in 2001 to $343 million in 2002.[38] As the FTC explained, these increases more likely reflect the Commission's success in casting a wider complaint net than they do a dramatic increase in fraudulent activity.[39] Nevertheless, improved reporting and complaint networks such as the FTC's *Consumer Sentinel* result in a more accurate, though still probably understated, picture of the extent of consumer fraud in the United States.[40] By far the largest category of reported incidents (43 percent) concerned identity theft, but substantial numbers of consumer fraud complaints concern Internet transactions and traditional areas of fraudulent activity such as credit protection, contests and sweepstakes, and business opportunity scams.

B. FALSE ADVERTISING

Advertising pervades modern commerce. False or misleading advertising is conceptually merely a category under the general area of deceptive practices. But because of the importance of advertising to most commercial firms, false advertising law has been the subject of extensive specialized litigation and rulemaking. The result is a well-developed body of law that furnishes guidance to firms seeking to avoid or manage the risk of false-advertising liability.

---

[37]   RESTATEMENT (SECOND) OF TORTS § 525 (1976).

[38]   Fed. Trade Comm'n, National and State Trends in Fraud and Identity Theft 3 (2002), *available at*   http://www.consumer.gov/sentinel/pubs/ Top10Fraud_2002.pdf.

[39]   *See* Press Release, Fed. Trade Comm'n, FTC Releases Top 10 Consumer Complaint Categories in 2002 (Jan. 22, 2003), *available at* http://www.ftc.gov/opa/2003/01/ top10.htm.

[40]   http://www.consumer.gov/sentinel (last visited Oct. 16, 2003).

This part of the chapter outlines the basic elements of liability for false advertising under the FTC Act, Section 43(a) of the Lanham Act, and most state UDAP statutes. Differences in standards between these bodies of law are noted where appropriate, especially on the topic of substantiation.[41] This part also discusses special recurring issues in false advertising that have been the subject of their own case law and rulemaking, including testimonials and endorsements, the advertising of prices, advertising as to the origin of a product, advertising that compares competing products, and disclaimers and disclosures.[42] Finally, possible First Amendment defenses to advertising challenges are discussed.[43]

1. Express and Implied Claims

False or misleading statements may be either express or implied. Where the statement is express, the meaning conveyed by the words of the statement itself must be deceptive before a claim will arise.[44] This seems straightforward enough. In practice, however, complications often arise. Analyzing whether express advertising is false or misleading requires the answers to a series of questions about the nature and scope of the statement being made.

First, what does the statement mean? Many advertising claims are susceptible to more than one interpretation. They may mean different things to different consumers or in the context of different other statements. As with virtually everything in advertising law, statements are assessed in the context of what else is said (and not said) in determining their literal meaning.[45]

Second, is the statement likely to be taken seriously? Exaggeration and hyperbole in advertising are as old as commerce itself and lend creative and humorous advertising much of its appeal. Advertising law credits consumers with a reasonable ability to distinguish statements that are meant in earnest from those that are not – the latter being known in advertising law jargon as "puffing."[46]

---

[41]   *See infra* 1.B.5.

[42]   *See infra* 1.B.8-12.

[43]   *See infra* 1.B.13.

[44]   *See* Castrol, Inc. v. Pennzoil Co., 987 F.2d 939, 941 (3d Cir. 1993).

[45]   *See* S. C. Johnson & Son, Inc. v. Clorox Co., 241 F.3d 232, 238 (2d Cir. 2001) ("[A] court must consider the advertisement in its entirety and not ...engage in disputatious dissection. The entire mosaic should be viewed rather than each tile separately.") (citation and internal quotation marks omitted).

[46]   *See* Pizza Hut, Inc. v. Papa John's Int'l, Inc., 227 F.3d 489, 496 (5th Cir. 2000), *cert. denied,* 532 U.S. 920 (2001) (finding that a claim is not

Third, can the statement reasonably be characterized as true or false? Statements about matters of taste, such as pleasant flavor or appearance, are inherently subjective and generally will not be found deceptive.[47] Statements of opinion – provided the opinions are accurately stated and, if attributed to someone, are truly held by that person – similarly are generally not open to challenge.[48]

Implied claims are claims not explicitly stated in the advertisement. Generally, they are claims that logically or naturally follow from, or provide a necessary premise for, claims that are explicitly made. More practically, an implied claim is any claim that the audience will understand the advertisement, taken in its totality, to communicate, even though the claim is not explicitly made.[49]

Some implied claims are more strongly implied than others. The strongest implied claims follow so naturally from express claims that are made that some courts treat them as if they were made expressly. These claims are said to be made by "necessary implication."[50] Other claims are more debatably implied, or perhaps implied to some consumers but not to others.

In Lanham Act cases, parties challenging an advertising claim on the ground that it conveys an impliedly false message – as opposed to an expressly false message – are required to present empirical proof of consumer deception.[51] Courts rarely enjoin advertising that is not

---

actionable unless it is "a specific and measurable claim, capable of being proved false"); Bose Corp. v. Linear Design Labs, Inc., 467 F.2d 304, 310-11 (2d Cir. 1972) (finding a claim that "countless hours of research" had produced a superior product to be nonactionable puffing).

[47] *See* Lipton v. Nature Co., 71 F.3d 464, 474 (2d Cir. 1995) ("Subjective claims about products, which cannot be proven either true or false, are not actionable under the Lanham Act") (internal quotation and citations omitted).

[48] *See* infra 1.B.8.

[49] *See* Johnson & Johnson-Merck Consumer Pharm. Co. v. Rhone-Poulenc Rorer Pharm., Inc., 19 F.3d 125, 132 (3d Cir. 1994).

[50] *See* Novartis Consumer Health, Inc. v. Johnson & Johnson-Merck Consumer Pharm. Co., 290 F.3d 578, 586-87 (3d Cir. 2002) (a "literally false message may be either explicit or conveyed by necessary implication when, considering the advertisement in its entirety, the audience would recognize the claim as readily as if it had been explicitly stated"); Clorox Co. v. Procter & Gamble Commercial Co., 228 F.3d 24, 34 (1st Cir. 2000); Castrol, Inc. v. Quaker State Corp., 977 F.2d 57, 62 (2d Cir. 1992).

[51] *See* Am. Brands, Inc. v. R. J. Reynolds Tobacco Co., 413 F. Supp. 1352, 1357 (S.D.N.Y. 1976) (holding that if a court confronts an advertisement involving "literally true or grammatically correct" statements, the trial

expressly false in the absence of consumer research.[52] As discussed below, the FTC and state enforcement agencies are more inclined than courts to rely on facial analysis to establish the existence of advertising claims even where the claims are implied.[53]

2. Omissions

Generally, under false advertising laws, advertisers are not required to state affirmatively or publicize things about their products or services, even when this information would be material to consumers.[54] However, under some circumstances, omissions are potentially actionable as a deceptive practice under the FTC Act or as false or misleading advertising under the Lanham Act. The conditions and standards relating to omissions differ between the two.

Under the FTC Act, the Commission regards an omission as deceptive if it makes it likely that reasonable consumers will be left with a false or misleading impression from the advertisement as a whole. This can happen in one of two ways:

1. the advertiser may tell a "half-truth" by making affirmative statements that are rendered misleading by the absence of further information that is omitted; or

2. the advertiser may remain silent "under circumstances that constitute an implied but false representation."[55]

---

judge cannot make a finding of deceptiveness unless the parties provide "evidence of substance" about what "the person to whom the advertisement is addressed find[s] to be the message").

[52] *See* McNeilab, Inc. v. Am. Home Prods. Corp., 501 F. Supp. 517, 525 (S.D.N.Y. 1980) (finding that evidence of consumer reaction "usually [takes]... the form of market research or consumer surveys"). However, a trial court may accord other forms of evidence "substantial weight" if that evidence appears reliable. *See* Am. Home Prods. v. Johnson & Johnson, 577 F.2d 160, 167 (2d Cir. 1978).

[53] *See* Kraft, Inc., 114 F.T.C. 40, 123 (1991), *aff'd,* 970 F.2d 311 (7th Cir. 1992), *cert. denied,* 507 U.S. 909 (1993). *But see* FTC v. Brown & Williamson Tobacco Corp., 778 F.2d 35, 40 (D.C. Cir. 1985) (ruling that the evidentiary value of consumer evidence on implied meaning of advertisement is the same under the FTC Act as under the Lanham Act).

[54] *See, e.g.,* Universal City Studios, Inc. v. Sony Corp. of Am., 429 F. Supp. 407, 410 (D.C. Cir. 1977). There are, however, many regulatory regimes beyond general false-advertising law that require specific affirmative disclosures in advertising relating to particular products or services, such as the various labeling statutes enforced by the FTC. *See* 16 C.F.R. §§ 300-314.

[55] Int'l. Harvester Co., 104 F.T.C. 949, 1058 (1984).

The second of these situations is deemed to exist if the advertiser fails to disclose issues that a reasonable consumer would take for granted if not disclosed, such as that a product is unfit for its intended purpose, is used, damaged, incomplete, defective, or hazardous.[56]

The Lanham Act standard regarding omissions reflects primarily the first of the two circumstances under which the FTC may consider an omission deceptive. "A failure to inform consumers of something, even something that they should know, is not per se a misrepresentation actionable under Section 43(a) of the Lanham Act."[57] However, the Act "protects against distortion through selective excerpting."[58] Thus, "a statement is actionable under § 43(a) if it is affirmatively misleading, partially incorrect, or untrue as a result of failure to disclose a material fact."[59] This does not mean that every material fact – under the Lanham Act definition, any fact likely to influence purchasing decisions – must be disclosed in every advertisement. Courts exercise discretion to determine which material facts, if omitted, render the advertisement false or misleading. In this determination, fact-finders treat the advertisement like any other advertisement, deciding whether, given the omission, claims in the advertisement are rendered literally false or false by implication.[60]

The most common challenges to omitted statements in Lanham Act claims occur when competitors allege that a comparison done against their product omits material facts that would weaken the apparent superiority of the advertiser's product.[61] For example, a pharmaceutical advertisement that criticizes a competitor for having side effects may be false or misleading if it omits mention of the advertised product's own comparably serious side effects.[62] However, any type of claim – or even visuals and other contextual material – can be held false or misleading if information necessary for a truthful depiction is not presented.

---

[56]   *See* FTC Deception Statement, supra note 28.

[57]   Pfizer, Inc. v. Miles, Inc., 868 F. Supp. 437, 449 (D. Conn. 1994), citing McNeilab, Inc. v. Am. Home Prods. Corp., 501 F. Supp. 517, 532 (S.D.N.Y. 1980).

[58]   Consumers Union v. General Signal Corp., 724 F.2d 1044, 1052 (2d Cir. 1983).

[59]   U.S. Healthcare, Inc. v. Blue Cross of Greater Phila., 898 F.2d 914, 921 (3d Cir.), *cert. denied,* 498 U.S. 816 (1990).

[60]   *See id.*

[61]   *Pfizer,* 868 F. Supp. at 450, citing E. R. Squibb & Sons, Inc. v. Stuart Pharm., Civ. No. 90-1178 (AET), 1990 WL 159909 (D.N.J. Oct. 16, 1990) and Oil Heat Inst. v. Northwest Natural Gas, 708 F. Supp. 1118 (D. Or. 1988).

[62]   *See E.R. Squibb,* 1990 WL 159909, at *18.

3. Materiality

The standard for materiality of an advertising claim has been fleshed out in FTC decisions and in case law. Under several common circumstances, there exists a presumption of materiality that is difficult to overcome. These circumstances include any instance where the alleged violator:

(1) made an expressly false claim;[63]

(2) should have known that the consumer needs information that was not disclosed;

(3) intended an implied claim; or

(4) made a claim in any of several areas generally established as relevant to consumers, including the purpose of the product or service at issue; its efficacy, quality or performance; health or safety issues; cost; durability; or a warranty.[64]

In the context of § 43(a) of the Lanham Act, a material fact is defined as a fact which, if known to purchasers, would likely influence the purchasing decision.[65]

4. Intent

Generally, no form of intent or knowledge of the falsity of an advertising claim is required for a finding of a false advertising violation. This is true whether the violation is of the FTC Act, the Lanham Act, or the majority of state UDAP laws. This comports with the fact that an injunction is the principal relief sought in most actions for false advertising, even where damages are permitted and are also sought. The law reflects the assumption that if an advertisement is false or

---

[63] *See* Energy Four Inc. v. Dornier Med. Sys., Inc., 765 F. Supp. 724, 731 (N.D. Ga. 1991); Alpo Petfoods, Inc. v. Ralston Purina Co., 720 F. Supp. 194, 213 (D.D.C. 1989), *aff'd in part, rev'd in part*, 913 F.2d 958 (D.C. Cir. 1990), *order modified*, 1991 WL 25793 (D.D.C. Feb. 8, 1991), *reh'g to recompute damages*, 778 F. Supp. 555 (D.D.C. 1991), *aff'd in part, modified in part, rev'd in part*, 997 F.2d 949 (D.C. Cir. 1993).

[64] *See* FTC Deception Statement, supra note 28; *see also* Novartis v. FTC, 223 F.3d 783, 787 (D.C. Cir. 2000); Thompson Med. Co. Inc., 104 F.T.C. 648 (1984), *aff'd*, 791 F.2d 189 (D.C. Cir. 1986) (holding that materiality can be presumed from a claim that a product is "new," implying greater efficacy than earlier products), *cert. denied*, 479 U.S. 1086 (1987).

[65] *See* NBA v. Motorola, Inc., 105 F.3d 841, 855 (2d Cir. 1997) (affirming dismissal of NBA's false-advertising claim because it was not "material," *i.e.*, "likely to influence purchase decisions"); U.S. Healthcare, Inc. v. Blue Cross, 898 F.2d 914, 922 (3d Cir. 1990).

misleading, it should be stopped, regardless of the intentions of the perpetrator.[66]

Intent does come into play in the area of damages. Many state consumer protection statutes provide for multiple damages (most frequently treble), minimum damages, and awards of costs and fees in cases where the defendant's misrepresentations were willful.[67]

Indirectly, intent is also implicated in some common exemptions under state laws. Most state UDAP statutes contain an exemption for printers, publishers, and other news media outlets that disseminate advertisements in good faith and with no knowledge that the advertisement is false or misleading.[68] Some exemptions are more limited, requiring that the exempted entity also have no financial interest in the advertisement.[69] In general, knowledge of the deceptive nature of the advertisement voids the exemption.[70]

5. *Substantiation*

The rules governing substantiation are the most important substantive difference between the FTC Act and most state UDAP statutes on the one hand, and the federal Lanham Act on the other. The FTC's position was outlined in its Policy Statement Regarding Advertising Substantiation, issued in 1983.[71] Under the FTC Act and

---

[66] *See* FTC v. Algoma Lumber Co., 291 U.S. 67, 81 (1934) (holding motive and knowledge of violation irrelevant to culpability under FTC Act); Porter & Dietsch, Inc. v. FTC, 605 F.2d 294, 309, (7th Cir. 1979), *cert. denied*, 445 U.S. 950 (1980) (same); M. Eagles Tool Warehouse, Inc. v. Fisher Tooling, 68 F. Supp. 2d 494, 506 (D.N.J. 1999) citing Brandt Consol. Inc. v. Agrimar Corp., 801 F. Supp. 164, 174 (C.D. Ill. 1992) ("The well settled rule is that there is no requirement under the Lanham Act that a false representation be made willfully or with intent to deceive. A mistake is not a defense to an action under § 43(a).") and Parkway Baking Co. v. Freihofer Baking Co., 255 F.2d 641, 648 (3d Cir. 1958).

[67] *See* Warner-Lambert Co. v. FTC, 562 F.2d 749, 763 n.70 (D.C. Cir. 1977), *cert. denied*, 435 U.S. 950 (1978); *see also infra* 3.B.2, 3.C.1.b.

[68] For example, such an exemption is contained in the UDTPA, § 4(a)(2), and is preserved in most state adoptions of the UDTPA.

[69] *See, e.g.*, People *ex rel.* Hartigan v. Maclean Hunter Publ'g Corp., 457 N.E.2d 480, 485-86 (1983).

[70] Thomas v. Times Mirror Magazine, Inc., 159 Cal. Reptr. 711, 715 (Cal. App. 1979); Mother & Unborn Baby Care, Inc. v. Texas, 749 S.W.2d 533, 538 (Tex. App. 1988), *cert. denied*, 490 U.S. 1090 (1989).

[71] *See* Fed. Trade Comm'n, Policy Statement Regarding Advertising Substantiation (1984), *available at*

most UDAP statutes, advertising that is not reasonably substantiated may be deceptive even if it is not proven false.   Indeed, advertising is deceptive under these statutes if the advertiser lacked substantiation at the time of making the claim, even if the claim is shown to be accurate subsequent to the dissemination of the claim, such as during the FTC's investigation or litigation.[72]   Under the Lanham Act, in contrast, advertising that is not ultimately found to be false or misleading is permissible, regardless of whether claims were substantiated at the time they were made.

a.   Substantiation under the FTC Act and State UDAP Statutes

Under the FTC's Policy Statement Regarding Advertising Substantiation, substantiation generally requires that one have a reasonable basis for any product claim at the time it is made. This is a flexible test that depends on several factors, including the type of product, type of claim, benefits of a truthful claim, cost and feasibility of developing substantiation, consequences of a false claim, and amount of substantiation that experts in the field believe is reasonable.[73]

In certain important and sensitive areas – chiefly claims relating to the health benefits or safety level of a product – the FTC goes further, requiring competent and reliable scientific evidence to support a claim. Such evidence includes "tests, analyses, research, studies, or other evidence based on the expertise of professionals in the relevant area, that have been conducted and evaluated in an objective manner by persons qualified to do so, using procedures generally accepted in the profession to yield accurate and reliable results."[74]

b.   Substantiation under the Lanham Act

Under the Lanham Act, substantiation generally is not required. Rather, a plaintiff must prove that the advertisement is false or misleading.   This is not merely a matter of burden shifting, but a difference in what is at issue in the two kinds of proceedings.   In a Lanham Act case, a defendant's *post hoc* showing that its claim was true when made – or the plaintiff's failure to prove that it was false – is a defense; under the FTC Act, it is not.

---

http://www.ftc.gov/bcp/guides/ad3subst.htm.   This position appears consistent with that taken by most states in adopting UDAP statutes.

[72]   Porter & Dietsch, Inc. v. FTC, 605 F.2d 294, 305 (7th Cir. 1979), *cert. denied*, 445 U.S. 950 (1980).

[73]   *See, e.g., In the Matter of* Pfizer, Inc., 81 F.T.C. 23 (1972).

[74]   *In the Matter of* Schering Corp., 118 F.T.C. 1030, 1127 (1994).

The one major exception to the rule that merely unsubstantiated advertising is not actionable under the Lanham Act pertains to establishment claims, discussed below. In addition, some courts in Lanham Act cases have held that a claim made in the complete absence of substantiation may be deemed literally false.[75] Plaintiffs challenging unsubstantiated advertising may fare better under state consumer protection statutes, many of which are based on the FTC Act and accordingly may prohibit unsubstantiated advertising as well as demonstrably false advertising. States specifically finding unsubstantiated advertising to be a UDAP violation, either by statutory provision or judicial decision, include California, Idaho, Iowa, Massachusetts, Missouri, and Ohio.[76] This list is likely not exhaustive of states whose courts would find unsubstantiated advertising unlawful in an appropriate case.

6. Establishment Claims

An establishment claim is an advertising claim that refers to evidence of the truth of the claims asserted.[77] Typical establishment claims include:

- "Three out of five doctors prefer Brand X."
- "Studies show that Brand X cleans better than Brand Y."
- "Brand X received the highest rating in product safety testing."

These claims represent not only that Brand X has a particular attribute, but also that there is evidence (probably scientific evidence) that Brand X has this attribute.[78] When such a claim is made, the claim

---

[75] *See* Sandoz Pharm. Corp. v. Richardson-Vicks, Inc., 902 F.2d 222, 228 n.7 (1990); Pharmacia Corp. v. GlaxoSmithKline Consumer Healthcare, L.P., 292 F. Supp. 2d 611, 621 (D.N.J. 2003); Accu-Sort Sys., Inc. v. Lazardata Corp., 820 F. Supp. 928, 932 n.7 (E.D. Pa. 1993).

[76] *See* People v. Custom Craft Carpets, Inc., 206 Cal. Rptr. 12 (Cal. Ct. App. 1984); IDAHO CONSUMER PROTECTION REGS., IDAPA 04.02.01.031; Iowa *ex rel.* Miller v. Hydro Mag, Ltd., 436 N.W. 2d 617 (Iowa 1989); IOWA CODE § 714.16(2)(a); MASS. REGS. CODE tit. 940, § 6.03(1) (2003); MO. CODE REGS. ANN. tit. 15, § 60-7.040 (2003); OHIO ADMIN. CODE § 109:4-3-10 (2003).

[77] *See, e.g.,* Johnson & Johnson Vision Care, Inc. v. 1-800-CONTACTS, Inc., 299 F.3d 1242, 1247 (11th Cir. 2002); C.B. Fleet Co. v. SmithKline Beecham Consumer Healthcare L.P., 131 F.3d 430, 435 (4th Cir. 1997); Rhone-Poulenc Rorer Pharms. Inc. v. Marion Merrell Dow, Inc., 93 F.3d 511, 514-15 (8th Cir. 1996); BASF Corp. v. Old World Trading Co., 41 F.3d 1081, 1090 (7th Cir. 1994); Castrol, Inc. v. Quaker State Corp., 977 F.2d 57, 62 (2d Cir. 1992).

[78] *See BASF*, 41 F.3d at 1090.

can be deemed false if the evidence described does not exist or if the advertisement has presented the evidence in a misleading way.

An establishment claim makes a representation about the product and, in addition, a representation about the existence and validity of certain evidence about the product. The underlying claim about the product may be true – Brand X may clean better than Brand Y – but claims of the type quoted above will still be deemed false if there are not studies showing that Brand X has the claimed qualities.

Establishment claims are generally held to convey, by necessary implication, not only that the referenced evidence exists, but also that it is valid and in accordance with generally accepted principles for gathering and analyzing such evidence.[79] For example, the claim that "Three out of five doctors prefer Brand X" cannot be substantiated by soliciting the opinions of just five doctors, three of whom prefer Brand X. Such a study would not meet scientific standards to generalize beyond the five doctors actually questioned. The "3 out of 5" claim conveys that competent research generalizable to some meaningful population of doctors has been done, and that roughly 60% or more of doctors surveyed voiced the opinion claimed by the advertisement.

7. Typicality

A claim or depiction of a product benefit or characteristic may be false or misleading if the benefit or characteristic is not typical of the performance of the product. The claim may also be false if the promoted benefit is true as to many or most consumers, but not true as to a substantial subset of consumers.[80]

8. Testimonials

Endorsements and testimonials rank among the most active areas of false-advertising litigation.[81] These are statements made in the context of an advertisement that the consumer is likely to believe reflect the opinion

---

[79]   *See Castrol*, 977 F.2d at 62-63.

[80]   *See* Tambrands, Inc. v. Warner-Lambert Co., 673 F. Supp. 1190, 1194 (S.D.N.Y. 1987) (finding "10-minute test" claim false for pregnancy test that delivered results in 10 minutes if results were positive, but took 30 minutes if results were negative).

[81]   *See, e.g.,* FTC v. Ken Roberts Co., 276 F.3d 583 (D.C. Cir. 2001) (challenging testimonials disseminated by investment research firms), *cert. denied,* 537 U.S. 80 (2002); Porter & Dietsch, P.C. v. F.T.C., 605 F.2d 294 (7th Cir. 1979), *cert. denied*, 445 U.S. 950 (1980) (challenging testimonials for weight-loss products).

or experience of someone other than the advertiser. The two terms may be regarded as synonymous for advertising law purposes, although in practice, "endorsements" generally more often denote a statement by a celebrity or recognized authority, while "testimonials" are often attributed to an anonymous person-on-the-street consumer.

The most useful single resource on this subject is the FTC's Guides Concerning Use of Endorsements and Testimonials in Advertising,[82] which sets the tone for FTC enforcement efforts, influences state courts' interpretations of many UDAP statutes, and may be taken as persuasive authority in Lanham Act cases.[83] The guides lay out the basic requirements for truthfulness in testimonial advertising.

First, the opinions expressed must be held honestly by the endorser.[84] The endorser's opinion may be edited, but not so as to change its meaning through distortion or omission.[85] Where celebrities are used as endorsers, this gives the advertiser a duty to check with the celebrity from time to time to verify that the opinions are still held.[86] Where paid actors speak as consumers, the actors should either be actual consumers who hold the opinions they are expressing, or the fact that they are paid actors must be clearly and conspicuously disclosed.[87]

Second, representations made by the endorser must comply with the other aspects of advertising law. If susceptible to a determination of truth or falsity – that is, if expressing something factual and not mere opinion – these statements must not be false or misleading.[88] An advertiser cannot get away with making untrue or unsubstantiated claims by having them come from the mouth of a consumer, even if the consumer honestly believes the statements.

Testimonials do permit some loosening of the typicality principle. If a consumer has had a bona fide experience with a product that is not typical of what a significant proportion of consumers could expect to experience, the consumer's experience may nevertheless be presented, as long as it is with a clear and conspicuous declaimer to this effect.[89] An

---

[82]   16 C.F.R. § 255.

[83]   *See, e.g.,* Diamond Mortg. Corp. of Illinois, 118 B.R. 583, 587 (Bnkr. N.D. Ill. Jul. 12, 1989) (interpreting Illinois Consumer Fraud and Deceptive Business Practices Act, ILL. REV. STAT., ch. 121 1/2 ¶ 261 et seq. (1987), recodified as 815 Ill. Comp. Stat. § 505/1 et seq. (2003); Ramson v. Layne, 668 F. Supp. 1162, 1165 (N.D. Ill. 1987) (same).

[84]   16 C.F.R. § 255.1(a).

[85]   16 C.F.R. § 255.1(b).

[86]   *Id.*

[87]   16 C.F.R. §§ 255.2, 255.5.

[88]   16 C.F.R. § 255.2.

[89]   *Id.*

adequate disclaimer in this situation either informs consumers that the depicted consumer's experience is not what the average consumer should expect, or (preferably) provides an indication of the true range of experience that consumers may expect.

Third, where an expert or authority is the endorser, the expert or authority must actually be qualified to evaluate the statement made about the product, and must be making statements relevant to that expertise or authority (although unrelated statements may be made as well).[90] Any implications created by the identity of the expert endorser, such as that it has conducted tests on the product to confirm its representation if it appears to be a testing organization, must also be truthful.

Finally, any relationship between the endorser and the advertiser that affects the endorser's credibility and is not ordinarily expected by viewers must be disclosed.[91] If the endorser is merely paid, this is expected by viewers and need not be disclosed.[92]

9. Price Advertising

Advertising related to pricing is one of the most extensively regulated of potentially deceptive practices, not only at the federal and state levels, but also by local governments. This is partly because the pricing of merchandise is often done at the local retail level in transactions that are entirely within, and therefore fall within the jurisdiction of, state and local authorities. It is also because advertising that one's product is a bargain is one of the most effective forms of promotion, creating incentives to deceive. Several types of price advertising that have become fertile ground for misconduct have become the subject of specific rules and holdings.

Once again, the FTC has taken the lead in mapping the terrain of this type of advertising violation, and the results are reflected in its Guides Against Deceptive Pricing.[93] The FTC has broken price advertising down into commonly seen categories.

a. Price Reductions

A claim of a price reduction implicitly or explicitly compares a currently offered price with a price formerly offered by the same seller. Deception in these claims generally involves quoting or implying an inflated, fictitious former price, so that what is actually the seller's

---

[90]   16 C.F.R. § 255.3.
[91]   16 C.F.R. § 255.5.
[92]   *Id.*
[93]   16 C.F.R. § 233.

regular price appears to be a reduction. Such claims are not deceptive if the former price was "offered to the public on a regular basis for a reasonably substantial period of time."[94] No sales need have been made at the former price.

b.   Price Comparisons

Comparisons of one's price against that offered by another are often an effective way of attracting customers. The FTC requires that the higher price attributed to the competitor, or to the market generally, must be the price actually offered by the competitor or a price at which substantial sales are being made in the same competitive area where the advertiser does business.[95] Comparing the advertiser's price to the manufacturer's suggested list price, for example, may be deceptive where almost no one in the same market is offering or selling the article at that price.[96] In addition, the product being sold by the advertiser must be the same as, or comparable to, the product being sold by the competitor whose price is cited.

c.   Other Price Advertising

The FTC also requires clear disclosure of the terms of deals in which a price is conditioned on the purchase of more than one item, or on some other action by the purchaser besides just buying the single product. This applies to promotions such as "two for the price of one," "free with purchase," or any other offer that would be deceptive, standing alone, if the additional requirements were not disclosed.[97]

State and local regulators often regulate other aspects of advertising, such as the means and prominence of the marking of prices on merchandise.[98] State laws may also impose additional restrictions on price advertising that go beyond those implied by the FTC Act. For example, some state advertising laws, regulations, or enforcement

---

[94]   16 C.F.R. § 233.1.

[95]   16 C.F.R. § 233.2.

[96]   Indeed, the FTC takes the view that discounting in many sectors has become so prevalent that advertising a price comparison against list or suggested resale prices is almost inherently suspicious.   16 C.F.R. § 233.3.

[97]   16 C.F.R. § 233.4.

[98]   Laws dictating the disclosure of prices are commonly termed "item pricing laws." *See, e.g.*, Albany County, N.Y., Item Pricing Law No. 1 (1992), *available at* http://www.albanycounty.com/departments/consumeraffairs/welcome.htm.

guidelines require that comparative retail pricing claims identify specifically the referent used as a basis for the price comparison.[99]

10. Product Origin

The FTC has a hand in administering several federal statutes governing the disclosure of U.S. versus foreign content in designated industries.[100]   For other products, the FTC has established rules governing whether "unqualified" and "qualified" claims of "Made in U.S.A." violate the FTC Act as deceptive practices.[101]

Unqualified made-in-U.S.A. claims are those that do not specify a partial or percentage U.S. content.   The FTC evaluates these claims under a flexible but strict standard that a product must be "all or virtually all" of U.S. origin to merit an unqualified claim.[102]   In making its determination in individual cases, the FTC considers primarily the percentage of the product's total manufacturing costs the can be assigned to U.S. versus foreign parts and processing, and the remoteness of any foreign processing from the final product.[103]   Final assembly of the product almost invariably must take place in the U.S., and so generally must the final production of any part of the product that makes up even a small, but significant, part of its cost.[104]

Qualified made-in-U.S.A. claims, such as "60 per cent U.S. content" or "made in U.S.A. of U.S. and imported parts," are examined more similarly to other advertising claims.   The FTC considers their literal and implied meanings and assesses whether these differ from the actual content and manufacturing process.[105]

Although less common, the same concepts and issues apply at the state level for products advertised as having been made within a state. Such advertising is popular to the extent that sellers wish to appeal to local consumers or to tourists.   Sometimes a state has a certain cachet

---

[99]   *See, e.g.,* MASS. REGS. CODE tit. 940, § 6.05(2) (2003).

[100]   *See* Textile Products Identification Act, 15 U.S.C. § 70; Wool Products Labeling Act, 15 U.S.C. § 68; Fur Products Labeling Act, 15 U.S.C. § 69. These statutes cover many other aspects of labeling besides designation of origin. *See also* American Automobile Labeling Act, 49 U.S.C. § 32304, which is not enforced by the FTC but which prescribes similar origin-related labeling for automobiles.

[101]   *See* FTC Enforcement Policy Statement on U.S. Origin Claims, 62 Fed. Reg. 63,756-01 (Sept. 2, 1997).

[102]   *Id.*

[103]   *Id.*

[104]   *Id.*

[105]   *Id.*

with respect to some product categories, such as Vermont maple syrup or Texas steak sauce. State Attorneys General can bring actions, as described below, under their Little FTC Acts or other consumer protection statutes for false designation of a product as being made in their state. For example, on March 10, 2003, the Vermont Attorney General announced a settlement with an Illinois company that allegedly falsely advertised its wood products as being made in Vermont.[106] The claim was brought under the Vermont Consumer Fraud Act's prohibition on unfair and deceptive acts and practices in commerce, and the challenged company agreed to modify its advertising and to pay the state an amount equal to all revenue that it had received from products it had designated as being made in Vermont, plus $1,000 to cover the Attorney General's costs.[107]

11. Comparative Advertising and Disparagement

When an advertisement highlights a shortcoming of a competitor's product, it may be false or misleading if it exaggerates the shortcoming or depicts effects of using the competitor's product that are not typical of that product's performance.[108] The FTC last restated its position on comparative advertising claims in 1979.[109] As with many FTC positions, it has been widely adopted or followed by legislators and courts.[110]

In general, comparative advertising is regarded as an especially useful source of information for consumers, and accordingly the FTC approves of comparative advertising in general and criticizes broad interpretations of state-law restrictions on "disparagement" of competitors that may chill this valuable commercial speech. Truthful criticism of competitors is thus encouraged. Indeed, the FTC has stated,

---

[106]   *See* Press Release, Vermont Office of the Attorney General, Attorney General Settles "Made in Vermont" Claims Against Wood Products Firm (Mar. 10, 2003), *available at* http://www.state.vt.us/atg/press03102003.htm.

[107]   *Id.*

[108]   *See* S. C. Johnson & Son, Inc. v. Clorox Co., 241 F.3d 232, 241 (2d Cir. 2001) (finding plastic food storage bag advertisement literally false where water was depicted leaking from competitor's bag at a rate experienced by very small percentage of competitor's bags).

[109]   FTC Statement of Policy Regarding Comparative Advertising, 16 C.F.R. § 14.15 (1979).

[110]   *See, e.g.,* Sony Computer Entm't Am., Inc. v. Bleem, LLC, 214 F.3d 1022, 1027 (9th Cir. 2000); August Storck K.G. v. Nabisco, Inc., 59 F.3d 616, 618 (7th Cir. 1995); Deere & Co. v. MTD Prods., Inc., 41 F.3d 39, 45 (2d Cir. 1994); Cumberland Packing Corp. v. Monsanto Co., 32 F. Supp. 2d 561, 581 (E.D.N.Y. 1999).

"[i]ndustry codes which restrain comparative advertising in this manner are subject to challenge by the Federal Trade Commission."[111] The FTC also rejects the application of any higher standard of substantiation or heightened scrutiny of allegedly deceptive claims on the basis that they are comparative or disparaging of another product.

Of course, the firm whose product is the subject of the negative comparison may not share the FTC's benevolent view. Comparative advertising therefore ranks among the most likely to provoke a challenge by a competitor, whether through the Lanham Act, a complaint lodged with the FTC, a challenge before a self-regulatory organization such as the National Advertising Division of the Council of Better Business Bureaus, or by a suit under one of the state UDAP laws that permits a competitor right of action.[112] For an advertiser, it often pays to take extra caution in limiting comparative advertisements to truthful and substantiated claims, notwithstanding that the FTC would treat them like any other form of advertising.

12. Disclaimers and Disclosures

One clear achievement of several decades of advertising law has been to increase the presence of disclaimers in advertising. "Fine print" disclaimers in print advertising are routine; television commercials involving complex, regulated transactions such as auto leases sometimes must devote most of the TV screen to disclaimers; and radio advertisers place a premium on announcers who can read disclaimers at speeds pushing the boundaries of comprehensibility. As intimated above, disclaimers serve several important legal purposes in advertising.

Disclaimers supply important details. A phrase such as "buy one, get one free," or "more cleaning power than Brand X," is almost inherently deceptive without additional information. The disclaimer usually will explain that a purchaser cannot get a $100 item free for buying a $5 item; the free item will typically be the lowest-priced one. Similarly, it may disclose that the superior cleaning power of the advertised product applies only to certain types of soiling, perhaps under certain conditions. The claims in these examples are neither wrong nor ambiguous, but by themselves they are incomplete. Disclaimers can prevent a finding that

---

[111]   16 C.F.R. § 14.15.

[112]   *See, e.g.,* Pharmacia Corp. v. GlaxoSmithKline Consumer Healthcare L.P., 292 F. Supp. 2d 594 (D.N.J. 2003); Pharmacia Corp. v. GlaxoSmithKline Consumer Healthcare L.P., 292 F. Supp. 2d 611 (D.N.J. 2003); McNeilab, Inc. v. American Home Prods. Corp., 848 F.2d 34 (2d Cir. 1988); U-Haul Int'l, Inc. v. Jartran, Inc., 793 F.2d 1034 (9th Cir. 1986).

the statements are deceptive because of the omission of important additional information, as discussed above.

Disclaimers can also clarify the meaning of an ambiguous statement. Where a literally true claim may be taken to imply a false claim to some consumers, an effective disclaimer may dispel any misconceptions. This can enable the claim to survive a challenge that it is impliedly false or misleading.

Advertisers cannot rehabilitate literally false claims simply by contradicting them with disclaimers. The same is probably true for claims that are false by necessary implication. The principle is that if an advertiser successfully uses a disclaimer to contradict a false claim, the making of the claim is pointless. Therefore, if an advertiser's disclaimer contradicts the main claim being made, one can deduce that the advertiser believes its disclaimer is ineffective and that a substantial part of the audience will understand and process only the false claim.

Disclaimers will be accepted only if they are "clear and conspicuous." The FTC and the courts do not evaluate the effectiveness of disclaimers standing alone; instead, they consider the entire advertisement, including the disclaimer, to determine whether a substantial proportion of the intended audience will likely perceive the deceptive message.[113]   In many instances, the FTC and/or courts reviewing claims under the Lanham Act and state UDAP statutes have established certain basic criteria for disclaimers, to ensure that they prevent false impressions. The examples of disclaimers described above, relating to the typicality of consumer experience with a product or the status of a paid endorser, find their roots in FTC pronouncements and existing case law.[114] Observance of these guidelines and precedents will help to establish a presumption that the final advertisement does not convey a misleading impression. Where no precise guidelines are available, the disclaimer is analyzed as part of the mix that conveys the overall impression of the advertisement.[115] Extrinsic evidence, such as experimental or survey data, may be necessary to prove (or disprove) the effectiveness of a disclaimer in a particular case.[116]

---

[113]   *See* FTC Deception Statement, *supra* note 28. The FTC and courts also recognize that advertising may be designed to draw the consumer's attention away from a disclosure or disclaimer. *Id.*

[114]   *See, e.g.,* Fed. Trade Comm'n, Guides Concerning Use of Endorsements and Testimonials in Advertising, 16 C.F.R. § 255, discussed *supra* at I.B.8.

[115]   *See* FTC Deception Statement, *supra* note 28.

[116]   *See generally* E&J Gallo Winery v. Gallo Cattle Co., 967 F.2d 1280, 1292 (9th Cir. 1992) (discussing survey evidence of effectiveness of disclaimer in § 43(a) trademark confusion case).

13. First Amendment Defenses

Injunctive relief awarded against advertisements and many commercial deceptive practices constitute prior restraints on speech, imposed or enforced by the government. As such, they raise issues regarding the Constitution's First Amendment protections of speech. [117] Two axioms govern the general analysis of the Constitutionality of a deceptive practice injunction. First, commercial speech is eligible for Constitutional protection, though not to as high a degree as political or "core" speech.[118] Second, *deceptive* commercial speech is *not* entitled to Constitutional protection.[119] The result of these two principles is that although Constitutional argument has a role in defending deceptive practices cases, it is a limited role and is not effective in the vast majority of cases.

The Federal Trade Commission has announced that:

> In executing our mission, we have found that the First Amendment commercial speech doctrine is fully compatible with our vigorous consumer protection program. The FTC requires that all claims be true, non-misleading, and substantiated at the time they are made. The FTC's post-market review of advertising claims and application of tailored remedies in advertising cases curb deception without overly restricting truthful commercial speech, thus promoting the goals embodied in the First Amendment.[120]

Nevertheless, the FTC concedes that it cannot determine with perfect accuracy which claims are false and which are true. Therefore, deceptive practices remedies must strike a balance between permitting commercial speech that may be false versus outlawing commercial speech that may be true.

The Supreme Court laid out a four-part test for the Constitutionality of government restraints on commercial speech in the *Central Hudson* case in 1980. Such restraints are Constitutional if the commercial speech concerns unlawful speech or is misleading, or if the commercial speech concerns lawful activity and is not misleading, but the government interest advanced is substantial, the regulation directly advances the

---

[117] Virginia Bd. of Pharmacy v. Virginia Citizens Consumer Council, 425 U.S. 748, 771 (1976).

[118] *Id.*

[119] *Id.*

[120] FTC Staff Comments, Request for Comments on First Amendment Issues, USFDA, Docket No. 02N-0209 (Sept. 13, 2002), *available at* http://www.ftc.gov/os/2002/09/fdatextversion.pdf.

governmental interest asserted, andthe regulation is not more restrictive than necessary to serve that interest.[121]

Where advertising claims have been found to be deceptive, the first part of this test justifies an injunction narrowly tailored to that claim.[122] The other factors come into play when broader relief is sought, including "fencing-in" injunctions, described in more detail below, that prohibit some truthful advertising or non-deceptive commercial activity along with practices that have been held deceptive. In such instances, the analysis passes to the other three factors.[123]

It has been established that the government has a substantial interest in restricting the dissemination of commercial speech that has the potential to mislead consumers.[124] Regulation of such speech, even if it is not entirely certain that the speech is misleading, may directly advance that interest. However, requiring disclaimers and additional disclosure is generally a less restrictive form of regulation than prohibiting the speech itself.[125] Therefore, these methods are Constitutionally favored unless the misleading claim is "incurable by disclaimer."[126]

By crafting its consent orders to avoid outright restraints and limit the scope of its prohibitions, the FTC has avoided First Amendment problems in its deceptive practices cases.[127] This success has put the

---

[121]   Central Hudson Gas & Elec. Corp. v. Public Service Commission of New York, 447 U.S. 557, 566 (1980).

[122]   *See id.* at 557.

[123]   *See, e.g.,* Bristol-Myers Co. v. FTC, 738 F.2d 554, 562-63 (2d Cir. 1984), *cert. denied,* 469 U.S. 1189 (1985) (finding fencing-in provisions constitutional as "reasonably related to the violation").

[124]   *See, e.g.,* Edenfield v. Fane, 507 U.S. 761, 769 (1993) (finding a substantial government interest in "ensuring the accuracy of information in the marketplace"). On the other hand, the government does not have a substantial interest in "preventing the dissemination of truthful commercial information in order to prevent members of the public from making bad decisions with the information." Thompson v. Western States Med. Ctr., 535 U.S. 357, 374 (2002).

[125]   *Thompson,* 535 U.S. at 376; *see also* Pearson v. Shalala, 164 F.3d 650, 658 (D.C. Cir. 1999), *reh'g en banc denied,* 172 F.3d 72 (D.C. Cir. 1999).

[126]   *Pearson,* 164 F.3d at 659.

[127]   *See, e.g.,* Bristol-Myers Co. v. FTC, 738 F.2d 554, 562 (2d Cir. 1984), *cert. denied,* 469 U.S. 1189 (1985); Sears Roebuck & Co. v. FTC, 676 F.2d 385, 400 (9th Cir. 1982); Litton Indus. v. FTC, 676 F.2d 364, 373 (9th Cir. 1982); United States v. Reader's Digest Ass'n, 662 F.2d 955, 965 (3d Cir. 1981), *cert. denied,* 455 U.S. 908 (1982); Jay Norris, Inc. v. FTC, 598 F.2d 1244, 1252 (2d Cir.), *cert. denied,* 444 U.S. 980 (1979). The single exception has been the invalidation of one provision in one

FTC in the position of advising other agencies that have not been so fortunate, such as the Food and Drug Administration, which solicited public comment on the issue after two cases in which the Supreme Court and the D.C. Circuit ruled that FDA actions with respect to advertising claims by pharmaceutical manufacturers were unconstitutional.[128] The FTC's response provides an instructive guide to the relationship between deceptive practices regulation and the First Amendment, as well as the FTC's enforcement philosophy.[129]

C. UNFAIR PRACTICES

Unfair business practices have only recently come to be regarded as something distinct from deception. At the FTC, unfairness took on a life of its own in 1980, with the FTC's Policy Statement on Unfairness.[130] In that statement, the Commission identified the factors in determining whether a business practices is unfair:

1. whether the practice, without necessarily having been previously considered unlawful, offends public policy as it has been established by statutes, the common law, or otherwise – whether, in other words, it is within at least the penumbra of some common-law, statutory, or other established concept of unfairness;
2. whether it is immoral, unethical, oppressive, or unscrupulous; [and]
3. whether it causes substantial injury to consumers (or competitors or other businessmen).[131]

The FTC considered these factors to have been approved by the Supreme Court in its 1972 decision in *FTC v. Sperry & Hutchinson.*[132]

The FTC regards the three unfairness factors as just that – factors, not elements that all need to be met for a practice to be unfair. Indeed,

---

[128] advertising consent order. *See* FTC v. Brown & Williamson Tobacco Corp., 778 F.2d 35, 45 (D.C. Cir. 1985).

[128] *Thompson*, 535 U.S. 357; *Pearson*, 164 F.3d 650.

[129] FTC Staff Comments, Request for Comments on First Amendment Issues, USFDA, Docket No. 02N-0209 (Sept. 13, 2002), *available at* http://www.ftc.gov/os/2002/09/fdatextversion.pdf.

[130] *See* Fed. Trade Comm'n, Policy Statement on Unfairness, *appended to* Int'l Harvester Co., 104 F.T.C. 949, 1070-76 (1980), *available at* http://www.ftc.gov/bcp/policystmt/ad-unfair.html [*hereinafter* "FTC Unfairness Policy"].

[131] *Id.* (quoting from Statement of Basis and Purpose, Unfair or Deceptive Advertising and Labeling of Cigarettes in Relation to the Health Hazards of Smoking, 29 Fed. Reg. 8324, 8355 (FTC 1964)).

[132] FTC v. Sperry & Hutchinson Co., 405 U.S. 233, 244-45 n.5 (1972).

the FTC stated that the third factor of substantial injury, alone – albeit the injury must be "unjustified," which perhaps incorporates elements of the other two factors – can support a finding of an unfair practice. Specifically, for the practice to qualify as unfair:

1. The injury must be substantial, generally involving monetary harm or health and safety risks, as opposed to, for example merely being offensive or tasteless. The injury also cannot be "trivial" or "speculative."

2. The injury must not be outweighed by any offsetting consumer or competitive benefits that the sales practice also produces. Thus, the Commission promises to take into account whether the practice complained of (e.g., not performing certain product testing) has certain proconsumer benefits (e.g., a lower price to consumers for the final product) and net out such benefits.

3. The injury must be one that consumers could not reasonably have avoided by, for example, purchasing a different product. Thus, the practice must be something that impairs a consumer's ability to avoid the injury, such as denying the consumer necessary information or employing overly coercive sales techniques.[133]

In 1994, Congress codified the FTC's unfairness definition by amending the FTC Act to specify that an unfair act or practice is one that "causes or is likely to cause substantial injury to consumers that is not reasonably avoidable and is not outweighed by countervailing benefits to consumers or competition."[134]

The violation-of-public-policy factor is vague, and in practice is used by the FTC to highlight the unscrupulousness of a challenged practice by demonstrating its inconsistency with the legislative or judicial history of other statutes. In its 1980 statement, the Commission averred that where it relies heavily on this factor to support a finding of unfairness, the policy "should be clear and well-established. In other words, the policy should be declared or embodied in formal sources such as statutes, judicial decisions, or the Constitution as interpreted by the courts, rather than being ascertained from the general sense of the national values."[135]

The unfair-and-unscrupulous factor is even more ambiguous, and even the FTC conceded that "[t]he test has proven...to be largely duplicative" of the other factors in the unfairness analysis.[136]

---

[133] FTC Unfairness Policy, *supra* note 130.

[134] 15 U.S.C. § 45(n).

[135] *Id.*

[136] *Id.*

Major FTC cases alleging unfair business practices are rare compared to deceptive practice cases. The FTC's most recent high-profile unfairness case started in 1997, when the Commission filed a complaint against R. J. Reynolds Tobacco Co., alleging that its marketing of Camel brand cigarettes using a cartoon mascot, "Joe Camel," was an unfair practice in that it caused children to take up smoking, leading to injury in the form of various health problems.[137] Nothing in the use of the Joe Camel character was alleged to be deceptive, in the sense of representing or implying any false or misleading messages. The use of Joe Camel was instead argued to be unfair because the attractiveness of the character to children would be excessively effective in persuading children to smoke cigarettes, short-circuiting their limited ability to decide this question rationally. Expressed thus, the Joe Camel theory fit the FTC's established definition of unfairness. The agency sought an order prohibiting Reynolds from advertising to children Camel cigarettes through the use of themes or images relating to "Joe Camel" and, as corrective measures, requiring that Reynolds disseminate public education messages discouraging persons under eighteen from smoking and that it collect data about the sales of its cigarettes to persons under eighteen.[138]

The FTC's case against Joe Camel was dismissed in 1999 because most of what the FTC sought was accomplished by the Multistate Settlement Agreement negotiated between cigarette manufacturers and state Attorneys General, who had sought compensation for tobacco-related public health expenditures.[139] This averted a ruling on what has become the central issue in most contested unfairness cases: evidence that the challenged practice "caused" the injury complained of. The FTC had voluntarily closed an earlier Joe Camel matter in 1994, when it concluded that, "Although it may seem intuitive to some that the Joe Camel advertising campaign would lead more children to smoke or lead children to smoke more, the evidence to support that intuition is not there."[140]

---

[137]   R. J. Reynolds, Docket No. 9285 (May 28, 1997) (FTC Complaint), *available at* http://www.ftc.gov/os/1997/05/d9285cmp.pdf. *See also* J. E. Villafranco & K. Saliba, *The Regulation of Fast Food Under the FTC's Unfairness Authority*, 228 N.Y.L.J. 4 (2002).

[138]   R. J. Reynolds, Docket No. 9285 (May 28, 1997) (FTC Complaint), *available at* http://www.ftc.gov/os/1997/05/d9285cmp.pdf.

[139]   R. J. Reynolds, Docket No. 9285 (Jan. 27, 1999) (Order dismissing Complaint), *available at* http://www.ftc.gov/os/1999/01/d09285.htm.

[140]   Joint Statement of Commissioners Mary L. Azcuenaga, Deborah K. Owen, and Roscoe B. Starek, III, R.J. Reynolds, File No. 932-3162 (June 6, 1994), available at http://www.ftc.gov/os/1997/05/rjrmla.htm.

Proving this causation presents a major obstacle for the FTC when it tackles mass-mediated advertising in an unfairness case. As described above, this is not a burden that the FTC or any challenger generally faces when alleging that advertising is false and misleading. Causation is generally much easier to show when the allegedly unfair practice is conducted one-on-one, such as through telemarketing or door-to-door appeals.[141] In such cases, the effects of the practice on individual consumers can be examined directly. With mass advertising, generally the only available means of proving causation of injury is by showing that the unfair aspects of the advertising campaign increased sales of the advertised product or service. Considering the many environmental factors that can cause increased or decreased sales, this can be a formidable task.[142]

Given these limitations, the unfairness doctrine is more useful against old-fashioned, one-on-one scams than against mass advertising. The Internet has proven to be fertile ground for such scams. Most of these scams are tantamount to consumer fraud, and it is under this doctrine that the FTC challenges bogus 900-number operations, pyramid schemes, and the proliferating forms of online cons. (The word "fraud" itself does not appear in Section 5 of the FTC Act.)

D. PRIVACY

The information society, much heralded since the 1960s, finally arrived in the 1990s. Despite decades of advance notice by futurists, certain parts of society soon proved to be unprepared. One unanticipated consequence of the high speed and low cost with which information can now be collected and disseminated is that entities, both private and public, have unprecedented capability to gather and use personal information about consumers. The legal system continues to struggle to catch up to these capabilities in formulating and enforcing rules to preserve some degree of consumer control over this information.

---

[141] Roscoe B. Starek III, *Unfairness, Internet Advertising and Innovative Remedies*, prepared remarks before the American Advertising Federation Government Affairs Conference (March 13, 1997), *available at* http://www.ftc.gov/speeches/starek/aaffin.htm. Mr. Starek was an FTC Commissioner at the time of his remarks.

[142] In such a case, the FTC generally also must overcome a defendant's First Amendment defense, which typically requires the Commission to show that the restraints it seeks to impose on speech will advance the goal of reducing consumer injury, *i.e.*, the advertising injunction will reduce sales of the product. Such evidence of prospective mass media effects is even more elusive than evidence of existing effects.

Legislative developments in the privacy area occur so rapidly that any fixed treatment of the subject, such as this one, necessarily has a short shelf life. As the most actively changing area of consumer protection law, privacy is the area where it is most essential for the practitioner to be familiar with current developments in the jurisdictions of interest. This section lays out the relatively stable principles and basic legal framework, focusing on federal privacy law.

The basic principle of privacy law is that consumers should be able to share personal information as needed to secure products and services that they want, such as loans, medical treatment, or the purchase of commodities, while restricting the use of that information for other purposes. At the very least, consumers should know to what use the collector may put that information prior to disclosure, so they can decide whether the desired product or service is worthwhile given the surrender of control over this information.

Disclosures to consumers regarding uses to which their personal information may be put are usually termed "privacy policies." The most basic and common privacy law issues are: (1) not having a privacy policy that is prominently disclosed to consumers and (2) having such a privacy policy but not abiding by it.[143] In addition, it is considered a violation of many privacy laws to collect information surreptitiously through technological means.[144]

Despite the active concern and legislative activity there is, as yet, no general federal statute specifically governing consumer privacy across commercial sectors. The issues described above are therefore generally reviewed by the FTC as potential deceptive practices under the FTC Act, and by state Attorneys General under their general consumer protection or UDAP statutes.[145] Legal attacks under these statutes are especially vigorous where privacy violations are entangled with other types of consumer fraud or deceptive practice. For example, scams that operate through telemarketing often rely on telephone number lists obtained by "information brokers" under false pretenses.[146] Privacy violations thus

---

[143] *Privacy Online: Fair Information Practices in the Electronic Marketplace, before the Senate Committee on Commerce, Science, and Transportation* (May 25, 2000) (prepared statement of Federal Trade Commission), *available at* http://www.ftc.gov/os/2000/05/ testimonyprivacy.htm.

[144] *Id.*

[145] Fed. Trade Comm'n, Privacy Agenda, *available at* http://www.ftc.gov/opa/2001/10/privacyagenda. htm (last visited Oct. 17, 2003).

[146] *Id.*

often go hand-in-hand with violations of the FTC's Telemarketing Sales Rule.[147]

The FTC has conducted high-profile investigations and litigations alleging deceptive practices relating to privacy violations, especially in the online area. These include:

- GeoCities. GeoCities entered into a consent decree to settle the FTC's charges that it misrepresented the purposes for which it was collecting personally identifiable information.[148]
- Eli Lilly & Co. Lilly settled FTC allegations that it disclosed, without authorization, sensitive personal information collected from users of its website promoting its Prozac product.[149]
- Microsoft Corp. Microsoft settled FTC accusations that it misrepresented the security of information gathered through its "Passport" web services.[150]

The most sensitive areas of personal information are considered to be financial and medical records. Accordingly, financial institutions and health care providers, as the creators and custodians of most of this information, are the subjects of extensive special privacy legislation. The Gramm-Leach-Bliley Act[151] is currently the main federal statute governing the use by financial institutions of consumers' personal information. It provides that financial institutions must disclose to customers their privacy and disclosure policies at the time of establishing a customer relationship, provide customers the opportunity to opt out of disclosure, and establish procedures to keep customer financial information secure.[152] The Act also outlaws "pretexting" – obtaining financial information from consumers under false pretenses.[153] The FTC enforces and has issued rules implementing the Gramm-Leach-Bliley Act.[154] In addition, the Fair Credit Reporting Act – one of several consumer credit statutes administered by the FTC – regulates the

---

[147]   16 C.F.R. § 310; *see also* Telemarketing and Consumer Fraud and Abuse Protection Act, 15 U.S.C. §§ 6101 *et seq.*

[148]   *See* GeoCities, Docket No. C-3850, 1999 WL 69858 (Feb. 5, 1999), *available at* http://www3.ftc.gov/os/1999/02/ 9823015.do.htm.

[149]   *See* Agreement Containing Consent Order, Eli Lilly and Co., File No. 012 3214, (Jan. 18, 2002), *available at* http://www.ftc.gov/os/2002/01/ lillyagree.pdf.

[150]   *See* Agreement Containing Consent Order, Microsoft Corp., File No. 012 3240 (Aug. 8, 2002), *available at* http://www.ftc.gov/os/2002/08/ microsoftagree.pdf.

[151]   15 U.S.C. § 6801.

[152]   *Id.*

[153]   15 U.S.C. § 6821.

[154]   13 C.F.R. § 313.

collection and disclosure of consumer financial information by credit bureaus.

In the health care area, the Health Insurance Portability and Accountability Act serves similar functions.[155] HIPAA requires that health plans and health care providers that transmit confidential patient information limit their disclosure to the "minimum necessary" to achieve the intended health care and that they obtain the consent of patients for most forms of disclosure.[156] Patients are also guaranteed access to their own medical records.[157]

Many privacy advocates, regulators, and enforcers focus on the Internet. Special privacy problems exist with the Internet because consumers have been more willing to provide personal information while on websites, without investigating the uses to which the information can be put, than they are in conventional transactions. The nature of "surfing" the Internet contributes to a casual approach and creates the illusion that what transpires on the screen is ephemeral. Businesses that gather information on the Internet, however, may be far from casual in compiling and using this information, and allegedly they provide less information about its gathering and use than traditional businesses. In addition, the Internet is popular among children and young adults who lack a sophisticated understanding of information security. Finally, Internet technology allows the use of devices invisible to the consumer, such as "cookies" – files stored on users' computers and accessed by Internet sites during future visits – that can potentially collect and disclose information without the consumer's knowledge or consent.

Internet privacy as it relates to children (persons aged under thirteen years) was addressed by the Children's Online Privacy Protection Act of 1998 (COPPA).[158] The FTC, charged with implementing and enforcing this statute, has issued a Trade Regulation Rule outlining enforcement intentions and guiding compliance.[159] COPPA is applicable to all commercial Internet websites that are targeted at children or that knowingly gather personal information from children.[160] Under COPPA, operators of such sites must provide notice about what personal information is being gathered, how it is used, and under what conditions it is disclosed by the operator.[161] This should be done through a prominent link to a page displaying the details of this privacy policy on

---

[155]   Pub. L. No. 104-191, 110 Stat 1936 (1996).

[156]   45 C.F.R. §§ 164.502(b), 164.514(d).

[157]   45 C.F.R. § 165.524.

[158]   13 U.S.C. §§ 1301.

[159]   16 C.F.R. § 312.

[160]   13 U.S.C. § 1303(a).

[161]   13 U.S.C. § 1303.

the site's home page and on each page where personal information is collected.[162]   Sites directed at children must also obtain "verifiable parental consent" to gather, use, or disclose personal information about children.[163]   The FTC assesses whether reasonable means have been taken to acquire verifiable parental consent based on a "sliding scale" that imposes a more rigorous requirement in cases where the website discloses children's personal information to third parties as opposed to using it internally.[164]

In addition, COPPA requires the site to honor the request of a parent to disclose to the parent what information has been collected from that parent's child, and to delete and cease to use that information.[165]   Parents must also be permitted to prohibit the disclosure of a child's information to third parties.[166]   Participation in activities on the site may not be conditioned on the child's provision of additional personal information not necessary to participate in those activities.[167]   Finally, sites are required to have reasonable means in place to protect the confidentiality of personal information collected from children.[168]

The FTC enforces COPPA aggressively.   In February, 2003, it settled charges of COPPA violations with Mrs. Fields Cookies and the Hershey Foods Corporation in which the two companies agreed to pay $100,000 and $85,000, respectively, in consumer redress for allegedly collecting information from children without first obtaining verifiable parental consent.[169]   The FTC also conducts sweeps of children's websites to assess COPPA compliance, and while it has found significant improvement from the dismal performance of 1998, before COPPA was

---

[162]   16 C.F.R. § 312.4.

[163]   16 C.F.R. § 312.5.

[164]   67 Fed. Reg. 18818 (Apr. 17, 2002). The sliding scale approach was intended to be a temporary expedient pending the wide availability of effective technologies for obtaining verifiable parental consent online. This technology did not develop as quickly as anticipated, and accordingly the sliding scale approach has been extended to April 21, 2005. *Id.*

[165]   13 U.S.C. § 1303(b)(1)(B).

[166]   *Id.*

[167]   13 U.S.C. § 1303(b)(1)(C).

[168]   13 U.S.C. § 1303(b)(1)(D).

[169]   United States v. Mrs. Fields Famous Brands, Inc., Civ. Action No. 03-CV-0205 (D. Utah, Feb. 27, 2003), *available at* http://www.ftc.gov/os/2003/02/mrsfieldsconsent.htm; United States v. Hershey Foods Corp., Civ. Action No. 03-CV-350 (M. D. Pa., Feb. 27, 2003), *available at* http://www.ftc.gov/os/2003/02/hersheyconsent.htm.

adopted, currently only about half of sites targeted at children are considered to be in compliance.[170]

The National Association of Attorneys General (NAAG) also has been active in the privacy area. NAAG has issued several reports critical of industry self-regulation efforts and urging various federal regulatory and enforcement agencies, including the FTC,[171] the Federal Communications Commission,[172] the Treasury Department,[173] the Federal Reserve System, the Federal Deposit Insurance Corporation, the Office of Thrift Supervision, the Office of the Comptroller of the Currency,[174] and the Department of Health and Human Services[175] to enact federal legislation relating to privacy or to step up enforcement efforts. However, the drafting of a general commercial privacy law – or even one regulating only online privacy – is a daunting task. While legislative efforts continue, privacy violations outside of specific regulated industries will continue to be pursued primarily as deceptive commercial practices.

In the meantime, Attorneys General, individually or in combination, have investigated and litigated privacy violations under their UDAP statutes. Major cases include actions against Internet advertising provider *DoubleClick* for failing to disclose its use of cookies, and

---

[170]   Fed. Trade Comm'n, Protecting Children's Privacy under COPPA: A Survey on Compliance 15 (Apr. 2000), *available at* http://www.ftc.gov/os/2002/04/coppasurvey.pdf.

[171]   *See* Comments of 44 Attorneys General to FTC Regarding GLB Notices (Feb. 15, 2002), *available at* http://www.naag.org/issues/pdf/20020215-signon-glb.pdf.

[172]   *See* Telecommunications Carriers' Use of Customer Proprietary Network Info., FCC Docket Nos. 96-115 and 96-149 (Dec. 21, 2001), *available at* http://www.naag.org/issues/pdf/20011228-signon-fcc.pdf.

[173]   *See* Comments of 36 Attorneys General on the GLBA Information Sharing Study Submitted [to the Treasury Department] *available at* http://www.naag.org/issues/pdf/20020502-multi-fin_info.pdf (last visited Oct. 20. 2003).

[174]   *See* Comments of 34 Attorneys General to the Federal Reserve System, the Federal Deposit Insurance Corporation, the Office of Thrift Supervision, and the Office of the Comptroller of the Currency Regarding Proposed Regulations Issued by the Agencies Under the Graham-Leach-Bliley Act, *available at* http://www.naag.org/features/glb_regs.pdf (last visited Oct. 20, 2003).

[175]   *See* Comments of 23 Attorneys General to the Department of Health and Human Services to Protect the Privacy of Medical Records, *available at* http://www.naag.org/legislation/Comments - AMENDED.pdf (last visited Oct. 20, 2003).

against retailer *Toys 'R' Us* for sharing cookie-collected information with the marketing company Coremetrics.[176]

While not a privacy statute in the same sense as the consumer-oriented laws discussed above, the Electronic Communications Privacy Act[177] bears on privacy rights in that it imposes duties to safeguard electronic information of any kind. The ECPA generally makes it unlawful to intentionally intercept most types of electronic communication between other parties, or to use or disclose information known to have been intercepted in violation of the Act.[178]

Further privacy legislation at both federal and state levels is inevitable, and the attorney who represents a client involved in the collection or disclosure of personally identifiable information must maintain a continuing surveillance of both legislative and judicial developments in this area.

---

[176]   *See* DoubleClick, Inc., AG File No. 200002052, State of Michigan, Department of Attorney General, Consumer Protection Division (Feb. 17, 2000) (Notice of Intended Action), *available at* http://www.michigan.gov/documents/dbleclck_43451_7.pdf; Press Release, New Jersey Dept. of Law & Public Safety, Division of Consumer Affairs, ToysRUs.com Enters Into Agreement with State (Jan. 3, 2002), *available at* http://www.state.nj.us/lps/ca/press/toysrus.htm.

[177]   18 U.S.C. §§ 2510 *et seq.*

[178]   18 U.S.C. § 2511.

CHAPTER 2

FEDERAL CONSUMER PROTECTION LAW AND ENFORCEMENT

Federal resolution of false advertising and deception claims occurs in two primary spheres: government actions by the FTC, and private litigation under Section 43(a) of the Lanham Act. Although the same false advertisement can attract unwanted attention from both of these sources, both the substantive law – as described above in Chapter 1 – and the procedural process differ substantially between the two.

The first part of this chapter describes the structure of the FTC's Bureau of Consumer Protection and the process by which consumer protection matters are handled by the Bureau. Reference is made to the regulations governing FTC practice and the various regulations, rules, and guides enforced or promulgated by the FTC, which are codified at Title 16, Chapter I, of the Code of Federal Regulations.[1]

The rest of this chapter examines private false-advertising litigation under Section 43(a) of the Lanham Act and summarizes the legal standards that have developed through Lanham Act case law.

A.   The Federal Trade Commission

The FTC quietly celebrated, in essence, its 100th anniversary on February 14, 2003. The Commission traces its ancestry to the Bureau of Corporations, then an investigatory unit of the Department of Commerce and Labor, founded in 1903 and renamed the Federal Trade Commission in 1915.[2] The Commission is headed by five Commissioners, each serving a seven-year term, who are nominated by the President and confirmed by the Senate. The President chooses one Commissioner to act as Chairman. No more than three Commissioners can be of the same political party. As of this writing, the current Chairman is Timothy J.

---

[1]   16 C.F.R. §§ 0.1-901.

[2]   *See* FTC Commemorates 100th Anniversary of Predecessor, Bureau of Corporations (Feb. 14, 2003), *available at* http://www.ftc.gov/opa/2003/02/ bcorp.htm. For an even deeper historical perspective, though one focusing on the FTC's competition antecedents, *see* Marc Winerman, *The Origins of the FTC: Concentration, Cooperation, Control, and Competition*, 71 ANTITRUST L.J. 1 (2003).

Muris, and the other Commissioners are Mozelle W. Thompson, Orson Swindle, Thomas B. Leary, and Pamela Jones Harbour.[3]

Structurally, the FTC is divided into three operational Bureaus – Consumer Protection (with which this volume is concerned), Competition, and Economics – as well as numerous other offices (including the Offices of General Counsel, Policy Planning, Congressional Relations, Public Affairs, the Executive Director, and the Inspector General). The Bureau of Competition is concerned with antitrust enforcement. The Bureau of Economics supports both the consumer protection and competition missions, although the nature of investigations and litigations in the two fields is such that the competition mission gives the Bureau of Economics the bulk of its litigation work. In the consumer protection area, however, the Bureau of Economics provides analysis of the likely economic impact of potential Commission investigations, litigations, and/or rulemaking, and is consulted on appropriate penalty levels to achieve the FTC's deterrence goals in consumer protection enforcement.

1. The FTC Act

Enacted in 1914, the Federal Trade Commission Act[4] brought the FTC into being in its present form. Originally the FTC Act was primarily an antitrust and trade regulation statute focused on unfair methods of competition; in 1938, however, it was amended to lay out the FTC's basic consumer protection agenda, giving the Commission broad authority to prohibit "unfair or deceptive acts or practices" in or affecting interstate commerce.[5] As further amended at various times, the Act has broadened but also refined the Commission's mandate, as discussed in more detail below. The current text of Section 5 of the FTC Act, which (among other things) sets forth the substantive provisions relating to consumer protection law, is reprinted in Appendix A to this volume.

2. Structure and Powers of the Commission in Consumer Protection Enforcement

The FTC's Bureau of Consumer Protection is divided into seven divisions.[6] Four of these are oriented to substantive areas of expertise.

---

[3]   For the current roster of Commissioners, *see* http://www.ftc.gov/bios/commissioners.htm.

[4]   15 U.S.C. §§ 41-58.

[5]   Act of March 21, 1938, ch. 49, § 3, 52 Stat. 111 (codified at 15 U.S.C. § 45(a)(1)).

[6]   *See* the Commission's website at http://www.ftc.gov/bcp/bcp.htm.

The Advertising Practices division examines deceptive and unsubstantiated advertising and is responsible for the Commission's high-profile activities in weight-loss and other nutritional or over-the-counter drug promotion, as well as all other forms of advertising. The Financial Practices division enforces several federal consumer credit statutes. The Marketing Practices division examines marketing practices other than advertising, ranging from get-rich-quick schemes to junk mail, and is the locus of the FTC's intensive activity in Internet fraud. The International Division's expertise lies in consumer protection issues that have an international component. These are supported by divisions that take specific roles in the investigatory, enforcement, advisory, or outreach practices. The Division of Enforcement conducts investigations, litigates, and enforces federal court injunctions and the Commission's consent orders. The Division of Planning and Information collects and analyzes data to support the Commission's other activities, including receiving consumer complaints. Finally, the Office of Consumer and Business Education operates public information campaigns for industry and the public. As described above, the Bureau is also supported by the FTC's Bureau of Economics for economic analysis relating to consumer protection matters.

a.   Enforcement Procedures

(1) Precomplaint Investigation

The FTC is empowered to "prosecute any inquiry necessary to its duties in any part of the United States"[7] (FTC Act Sec. 3, 15 U.S.C. Sec. 43) and to "gather and compile information concerning, and…investigate from time to time the organization, business, conduct, practices, and management of any person, partnership, or corporation engaged in or whose business affects commerce," with certain exceptions (primarily financial institutions and common carriers) that are closely overseen by other agencies.[8]   The existence of an FTC investigation is usually, but not always, considered nonpublic. However, the FTC does announce some investigations in press releases at its discretion, and leaks also may occur. Thus, confidentiality exists as a general rule but cannot be relied upon.

In the course of an investigation, the FTC's Bureau of Consumer Protection generally issues Civil Investigative Demands (CIDs), devices

---

[7]   15 U.S.C. § 43.
[8]   15 U.S.C. § 46(a).

similar to, but broader than, traditional discovery subpoenae.[9] Under a CID, the Commission may require not only the appearance and testimony of witnesses and/or the production of any documents or tangible things relevant to the inquiry, but also (or alternatively) that the recipient "file written reports or answers to questions."[10] The recourse of a recipient of a CID is to file a motion to quash it in any U.S. district court where jurisdiction and venue are appropriate; by the same token, the Commission may avail itself of any such district court to enforce the CID in the event of noncompliance.[11]

The FTC is also empowered to require entities to submit and file "annual or special…reports or answers in writing to specific questions" for the purpose of obtaining "information about the organization, business, conduct, practices, management, and relation to other corporations, partnerships, and individuals" to whom the inquiry is addressed.[12] These are more comprehensive reports than are contemplated by the requirement to generate documents or reports under an investigative CID. Their objective is to require participants in a business or operation under investigation to provide the FTC with a regular and general account of their activities. The FTC can synthesize these reports into broad economic studies of an entire industry. As with a CID, a request for such a special report may be challenged by a recipient through a motion to quash or enforced by the FTC through a contempt proceeding in a federal district court.[13] The FTC is authorized, at its discretion, to make public the information received in response to these requests.[14]

In practice, FTC investigations combine these formal investigatory devices with informal meetings and discussions between the FTC staff and the entities involved in the investigation. Staff may make requests for voluntary access prior to issuing a CID.[15] Upon receiving a CID, a recipient generally contacts the FTC staff attorney who sent the demand, seeking to negotiate a mutually acceptable timetable for production of documents and witnesses and to delineate any questions that cannot

---

9   15 U.S.C. § 57b-1. The Bureau of Competition, which operates the FTC's antitrust "mission," additionally may issue subpoenae. 15 U.S.C. § 49. However, since 1980, this device has not been available to the Bureau of Consumer Protection at the precomplaint stage.

10   15 U.S.C. § 57b-1(c)(1).

11   16 C.F.R. § 2.13.

12   15 U.S.C. § 46; 16 C.F.R. §2.12.

13   16 C.F.R. §2.13.

14   15 U.S.C. § 46(f).

15   FTC Operating Manual ch. 1.3.4.1, *available at* http://www.ftc.gov/foia/adminstaffmanuals.htm.

feasibly be answered. In addition, other entities that have not received a CID may be in touch with the FTC. Some investigations are triggered by complaints made by one or more competitors, customers, or other entities, who may continue to supply information over the course of the investigation. The FTC may also initiate contact with other entities on an informal basis.

(2) Sting Operations

The FTC periodically launches sting operations targeting a group of prospective defendants in an area where deceptive practices are deemed to be rampant. To take a representative recent example, in 2002 the FTC launched Project Busted Opportunity, an undercover sting operation targeting purveyors of business opportunity programs that the FTC suspected of committing deceptive acts and practices, and more specifically of violating the disclosure requirements of the FTC's Franchise Rule.[16] The FTC used undercover investigators posing as customers to unearth numerous alleged misrepresentations relating to the marketing of these opportunities.[17] Filing complaints initially in June, 2002, the FTC continued to amend its complaint to add more defendants. By January, 2003, the FTC claimed that seventy-seven "operations" had been caught in the sting.[18]

In these and other enforcement efforts, the FTC frequently cooperates with other law enforcement agencies at the federal and state levels, and with consumer groups. In Project Busted Opportunity, for example, the seventeen groups that cooperated with the FTC included state and local Better Business Bureaus, state Attorneys General, and local police departments, several of which filed their own separate legal actions against entities targeted in the sting operation.[19]

(3) Adjudicative Procedures

When the Commission decides that it has "reason to believe" that the law is being violated and that the time has come to file a complaint, it has two options. Under Part 3 of the FTC Rules of Practice, the FTC may file for administrative adjudication or, under Section 13(b) of the FTC Act, it may file a complaint in federal court.[20] Both methods continue to

---

[16]   *See* TRADE REG. REP. (CCH) ¶ 15,270 (Dec. 4, 2003).
[17]   *Id.*
[18]   *Id.*
[19]   *Id.*
[20]   *See* 15 U.S.C. §53(b); 16 C.F.R. §3.2.

be used by the Commission, although in the consumer protection area, the focus has shifted to federal court over the past twenty years.[21]

No written policy guides the Commission's decisions on venue. The benefits to the federal court approach include the wide variety of equitable remedies available, discussed below, as well as the speed with which remedies such as temporary restraining orders, preliminary injunctions, and asset freezes can be obtained. This is especially valuable when dealing with the traditional fly-by-night huckster operation, whose principals and assets can prove elusive if they are given much time to hide or escape.

(a) ADMINISTRATIVE TRIALS

FTC administrative trials are adjudicated before an Administrative Law Judge (ALJ) under the Commission's Rules of Practice.[22] FTC staff attorneys prosecute the case before the ALJ, whose docket consists only of FTC cases. At the conclusion of a trial-like hearing, the ALJ issues an initial decision setting forth his or her findings of fact and conclusions of law, and recommending either dismissal of the case or a cease-and-desist order.[23] Either party, if unhappy with this recommendation, may appeal to the FTC Commissioners.[24]

If the initial decision is appealed, the Commissioners hold an appellate-like hearing – again under the FTC's Rules of Practice – culminating in a final decision and order.[25] On appeal, cases before the Commission are reviewed de novo.[26] A respondent wishing to appeal this final order may file a petition for review with any court of appeals within whose jurisdiction the respondent "resides or carries on business or where the challenged practice was employed."[27] Thus, the Circuit Court of Appeals, in a third round of litigation, is generally the first federal court to which the respondent has access if the FTC has elected to file an administrative complaint. The Court of Appeals may affirm or

---

[21] James P. Timony, Administrative Adjudication of Consumer Protection Cases as an Alternative to Litigation in Federal Court, CONSUMER PROTECTION UPDATE (ABA Section of Antitrust Law Consumer Protection Committee Newsletter), at 2-3 (Fall 2002), *available at* http://www.abanet.org/antitrust/committees/consumer/cpfall02.pdf.

[22] 16 C.F.R. §§ 3.1 *et seq.* govern the conduct of the FTC's administrative trials.

[23] 16 C.F.R. § 3.51.

[24] 16 C.F.R. § 3.52.

[25] 16 C.F.R. § 3.54.

[26] 16 C.F.R. § 3.54(a).

[27] 15 U.S.C. § 45(c).

reverse the Commission's order. However, the Court of Appeals is required to consider that "findings of the Commission as to the facts, if supported by evidence, shall be conclusive."[28] Courts have interpreted this standard as meaning that the Commission's factual findings must be supported by "substantial evidence," a standard that, in practice, is still very deferential.[29] Ultimate recourse by either side is to the U.S. Supreme Court.

Administrative trials have undergone a gradual evolution during the history of the FTC. Starting as a very limited proceeding in which the few permissible pleadings, discovery, and adjudication were compressed into a single hearing, the FTC administrative adjudication process has come to borrow many procedural practices from federal civil litigation, with the ultimate hearing before the ALJ resembling a civil bench trial.[30] These changes also lengthened the proceedings, ultimately to the point that, in 1996, the FTC instituted major changes designed to render its administrative proceedings substantially faster than civil trials.[31] Under the new rules, the ALJ is required to issue the initial decision within one year of the issuance of the FTC's complaint, with correspondingly compressed deadlines for discovery.[32]

The Commission also established an alternative "fast track" schedule that respondents may elect when the Commission has filed for a preliminary injunction in a collateral federal court proceeding and either has been granted the injunction or determines that the federal court proceeding has created an adequate factual record for fast-track resolution at the Commission. Under the fast-track procedure, the ALJ's initial ruling is to be entered within 195 days of the issuance of the injunction or other "triggering event," and the Commission's final order and opinion is to be issued within thirteen months.[33] In addition, new rules imposing tighter deadlines were established seeking to minimize discovery and trial delays. In 2001, several more amendments were made, including an electronic filing requirement.[34]

---

[28] *Id.*

[29] *See* Corn Prods. Ref. Co. v. FTC, 324 U.S. 726, 739 (1945); FTC v. A.E. Staley Mfg. Co., 324 U.S. 746, 758 (1945).

[30] *See* D. Bruce Hoffman & M. Sean Royall, Administrative Litigation at the FTC: Past, Present, and Future, 71 ANTITRUST L.J. 319 (2003).

[31] A full summary of the 1996 rules changes is available at http://www.ftc.gov/os/1996/09/part3rul.htm.

[32] 16 C.F.R. § 3.51(a).

[33] 16 C.F.R. § 3.11A.

[34] 16 C.F.R. § 4.2. A full summary of the 2001 amendments is available at http://www.ftc.gov/os/2001/03/rpamend.htm

The FTC claims to see certain advantages in administrative adjudication.[35] First, the Commission is on its "home turf" in such a proceeding and, although ALJs do a creditable job of being impartial, the FTC's track record in adjudicative proceedings is impressive. Ultimately, the Commissioners are empowered to review the ALJ's finding *de novo,* reinforcing the FTC's dual role of both prosecutor and judge.[36] Even more importantly, administrative adjudication confers advantages on the FTC on appeal before a Circuit Court. As described above, such a court must affirm the Commission's findings of fact if supported by "substantial evidence." It must also accord "substantial deference" to the Commission's interpretations of the FTC Act and of its own rules.[37] The FTC would not enjoy such advantages in a suit brought in federal court, where the familiar standards of review (i.e., clearly erroneous as to findings of fact; *de novo* as to conclusions of law) apply. As the FTC puts it, "where a case involves novel legal issues or fact patterns, the Commission has tended to prefer administrative adjudication."[38] In sum, administrative adjudication sharply limits the forms of relief available to the FTC and can take a long time, but the "home court" and general deference afforded to the Commission on appeal are attractive benefits in cases where the outcome is uncertain.

A Commission order at the end of an administrative proceeding becomes final sixty days after it is served;[39] consent orders, at the Commission's discretion, are effective immediately upon service.[40] The FTC normally requires respondents to submit regular compliance reports documenting compliance with the order.[41] If the FTC deems the respondent not to be in compliance, it may sue in a federal district court to enforce compliance with the order, as well as for additional injunctive and equitable relief if the court deems these appropriate.[42] The potential civil penalty for violating an FTC order is up to $11,000 per violation.[43] Each continuing instance of a violation is deemed to be a new violation

---

[35]   *See* A Brief Overview of the Federal Trade Commission's Investigative and Law Enforcement Authority (Sept., 2002), *available at* http://www.ftc.gov/ogc/brfovrvw.htm.

[36]   Hoffman & Royall, *supra* note 30, at 320.

[37]   *See* Firestone Tire & Rubber Co. v. FTC, 481 F.2d 246, 248-49 (6th Cir. 1973), *cert. denied,* 414 U.S. 1112 (1974).

[38]   *See* supra note 35.

[39]   16 C.F.R. § 3.56.

[40]   16 C.F.R. §§ 2.32, 2.34.

[41]   16 C.F.R. § 2.41.

[42]   15 U.S.C. § 45(l).

[43]   16 C.F.R. § 1.98(c).

for which an additional $11,000 can be recovered, leading to the possibility of very large penalties in many cases.

FTC orders typically provide for an injunction against the challenged conduct. The FTC can and often does also go further than this by including order provisions that enjoin related conduct that is not necessarily violative of the FTC Act. Known as "fencing-in" provisions, these prohibitions are based on the principle that the violator cannot be trusted to undertake even certain lawful activities, lest he find a way to repeat or better conceal his deceptive practices in the future.[44] As a typical example, owners of telemarketing companies who are found to have committed major violations are often barred from any future involvement in telemarketing.[45]

Once an order is final, the Commission may yet seek consumer redress from the respondent in district court for consumer injury caused by the conduct addressed by the order. The standard for recovery by the Commission in such cases is whether "a reasonable man would have known under the circumstances [that the respondent's conduct] was dishonest or fraudulent."[46]

The FTC may also employ the final order from an adjudicatory proceeding to attack the same conduct by other entities that were not named in the original investigation or proceeding, without having to re-litigate the issue of whether the challenged conduct is deceptive. Where the conduct is the same as that challenged in the proceeding, the FTC need only show that the new violator had "actual knowledge that such act or practice is unfair or deceptive and is unlawful" under Section 5(a)(1) of the FTC Act in order to obtain immediate civil penalties in federal court.[47] In practice, this standard is met if the FTC itself has sent the violator a copy of the final order in question.

(b) Actions in Federal District Court

The FTC's powers were significantly expanded by the addition of Section 13(b) to the FTC Act in 1973.[48] Under this section, the FTC may

---

[44] *See* FTC v. Ruberoid Co., 343 U.S. 470, 473 (1952) (explaining that the Commission is not limited to prohibiting the illegal practice alone, but can block "all roads to the prohibited goal, so that its order may not be passed by with impunity").

[45] *See, e.g.*, FTC v. 1st Beneficial Credit Servs., Docket No. 1:02CV1591 (N.D. Ohio Sept. 19, 2003), *available at* http://www.ftc.gov/os/2003/09/firstbenefitstip.pdf.

[46] 15 U.S.C. § 57b.

[47] 15 U.S.C. § 45(m)(1)(B).

[48] 15 U.S.C. § 53(b).

seek equitable relief, including preliminary and/or permanent injunctions, against violators of the FTC Act in federal court. Most courts interpret the provision as allowing the FTC to pursue the full range of equitable remedies in these actions.[49] Equitable remedies sought and secured by the FTC in federal court actions, either by judgment or by settlement and consent decree, include consumer redress running into the tens and sometimes hundreds of millions of dollars, either through judgments or settlements.[50] Additional remedies include temporary restraining orders, freezing of assets, and appointment of receivers.[51]

The monetary equitable relief available to the FTC falls into accepted categories, such as restitution and disgorgement, collectively termed "consumer redress" by the Commission. In the case of the restitution remedy, funds paid by the consumer are ordered to be repaid to them by the offender.[52] This form of redress is common in fraud cases, where consumers who were taken in by the scam can be identified readily, but obviously is not practical in false advertising cases. In the latter, the typical remedy is disgorgement of the violator's ill-gotten profits to the FTC.[53] Disgorgement is often also applied as an additional

---

[49] *See* FTC v. Southwest Sunsites, Inc., 665 F.2d 711, 717-18 (5th Cir. 1982), *cert. denied*, 456 U.S. 973 (1983); FTC v. H. N. Singer, Inc., 668 F.2d 1107, 1113 (9th Cir. 1982).

[50] *See, e.g.*, FTC v. Access Res. Servs., Inc., Docket No. 02-60226-CIV (S.D. Fla. Nov. 4, 2002) (settling for $500 million in redress), *available at* http://www.ftc.gov/opa/2002/11/ars.htm; FTC v. Citigroup, Inc., 2002-1 Trade Cas. (CCH) ¶ 73,529 (N.D. Ga. 2001) (settling for $200 million in redress); FTC v. First Alliance Mortgage Co., Docket No. SACV-00-964 DOC (EEx) (C.D. Cal. March 21, 2002) (settling for $65 million in redress), *available at* http://www.ftc.gov/opa/2002/03/famco.htm; FTC v. Windermere Big Win Int'l, Civ. Act. No. 98 C 8066 (N.D. Ill. Oct. 23, 2000) (ordering payment of $19 million in consumer redress), *available at* http://www.ftc.gov/opa/2000/10/windermere.htm.

[51] *See, e.g.*, FTC v. Trek Alliance, Inc., Docket No. CV-02-9270 SJL (AJWx) (C.D. Cal. Dec. 16, 2002) (awarding TRO, freezing of assets, and temporary receiver), *available at* http://www.ftc.gov/opa/2002/12/trek.htm.

[52] *See, e.g.*, FTC v. Alyon Techs., Inc., Docket No. 1:03-CV-1297-RWS (N.D. Ga. July 16, 2003) (ordering defendant to pay restitution to consumers that protested illegal billing) *available at* http://www.ftc.gov/opa/2003/07/alyon01.htm.

[53] *See, e.g.*, FTC v. SlimAmerica, Inc., 77 F. Supp. 2d 1263 (S.D. Fla. 1999) (ordering disgorgement of company's total sales for falsely advertising weight loss product).

"kicker" in cases where restitution is ordered, because it is unlikely that all affected consumers are successfully being identified and fully repaid.

In some cases, affirmative equitable relief may also be required. These measures are especially useful in cases of false advertising. Violators may be forced to include disclosures in future advertising. They may be required to create and disseminate corrective advertising designed to help correct the misimpressions that their past advertising has created.[54] They may also be required to fund public education campaigns to help undo the damage.[55]

The FTC's ability to pursue actions directly in federal court has great advantages, especially for shutting down the garden-variety hucksters that provide much of the Consumer Protection division's day-to-day workload. The merits of these scams are not exotic, and there is no great need to educate a generalist federal court about what makes the conduct unfair or deceptive. The court can move quickly to shut down the offender before it slips through the cracks. It can also deploy all of the tools of equity to obtain both injunctive and monetary forms of equitable relief in a single proceeding, whereas otherwise the FTC would have to go through the adjudicative process and then resort to a federal court action to gain the same relief.

(4) Settlement

The FTC encourages settlement of consumer protection matters both before and after the filing of a complaint. Because of the drain litigation places on the FTC's limited resources, and as a matter of general policy, serious settlement overtures to the Commission staff are usually met with a ready ear. All of the forms of relief available to the Commission in either administrative proceedings or federal court, as discussed below, are also typical features of consent orders negotiated with the FTC.

Settlements of FTC investigations and suits result in consent orders. These are reached through a negotiation process in which respondents attempt to persuade the FTC of the defects in its case, and both sides will exchange iterative proposals for relief. Once a consent order is agreed

---

[54]   *See, e.g.*, Novartis v. FTC, 223 F.3d 783, 788 (D.C. Cir. 2000) (upholding order requiring corrective advertising); Warner Lambert Co. v. FTC, 562 F.2d 749, 762 (D.C. Cir. 1977), *cert denied*, 435 U.S. 950 (1978).

[55]   *See, e.g., In the Matter of* Schering-Plough Healthcare Prods. Inc., 123 F.T.C. 1301 (1997) (in consent decree, requiring defendant to produce and distribute 150,000 consumer education brochures regarding sunscreen protection for children after making allegedly unsubstantiated claims regarding effectiveness of its sunscreen product).

upon, the FTC publishes the proposed order for thirty days of public comment before determining whether to make the order final.[56]

Consent orders reached with the FTC contain no admission of liability by the respondent. However, the orders are made public, and readers are free to draw their own conclusions from the type of relief agreed upon. In addition, the issuance of the consent order is accompanied by a complaint, an FTC press release, an analysis to aid public comment, and in some cases, a press conference. The FTC's policy is not to reach agreements with respondents on what is said in these materials, and in practice, the FTC often goes well beyond the terms of the consent order in these statements. Often the materials proclaim the guilt of the respondent as if the FTC had won a litigation victory, and sometimes they cite a speculative monetary amount that the respondent has allegedly cost consumers through its deceptive practices.[57] As a practical matter, the respondent's press release often will not be as widely quoted as the FTC's announcements, leaving the respondent without a full opportunity to respond to the Commission's allegations. Often more importantly, speculative damage figures quoted by the FTC can quickly reach the attention of class action plaintiffs and counsel, leading to follow-on private litigation under state UDAP statutes.[58]

b. Other Statutes Enforced by the FTC

Over the decades, the FTC has been instrumental in bringing about many of the statutes that make up the modern system of business regulation in the U.S. through its research, investigations, and other actions. These include statutes such as the Securities Act of 1933[59] that the FTC no longer actively administers. The FTC does, however,

---

[56]   16 C.F.R. § 2.34(c).

[57]   *See, e.g.,* Press Release, Fed. Trade Comm'n, Fraudulent Canadian Credit Card Operation Permanently Halted (June 2, 2003), *available at* http://www.ftc.gov/opa/2003/06/uscredit.htm.

[58]   *See, e.g., Laraia v. Rexall Sundown, Inc.,* Case No. CL 00 7021 AF (Fla. Cir. Ct. August 9, 2002) (certifying nationwide class, except for California where separate suit had been filed, in false advertising case following FTC action). In some cases, as in Rexall, the FTC conditions its own settlement on the approval by courts of satisfactory settlements in the follow-on private actions. *See FTC v. Rexall Sundown, Inc.,* Case No. 00-7016-CIV-MARTINEZ (S.D. Fla.) (stipulated final order filed March 11, 2003), *available at* http://www.ftc.gov/os/2003/03/rexallstiporder.htm.

[59]   17 U.S.C. §§ 77a-77mm.

enforce the following types of consumer-oriented statutes. The list below is not exhaustive, but conveys the general range of consumer-related laws that the FTC is charged with implementing and enforcing.

Credit-Related Laws. The FTC enforces the Truth in Lending Act,[60] the Fair Credit Billing Act,[61] the Fair Credit Reporting Act,[62] the Equal Credit Opportunity Act,[63] and the Fair Debt Collection Practices Act.[64] These acts require a wide variety of disclosures and practices relating to various forms of extension of credit to consumers.

Laws Governing Other Financial Consumer Transactions. The FTC also enforces the Consumer Leasing Act[65] and the Electronic Fund Transfer Act,[66] which govern the rights and liabilities of parties to these common consumer transactions.

Warranties. The FTC enforces the Magnuson-Moss Warranty Act.[67] Under this Act, the FTC establishes disclosure and designation standards for written warranties, specifies standards for full warranties, and establishes consumer remedies for breach of warranty or service contract obligations.

Packaging and Labeling. The FTC enforces the Fair Packaging and Labeling Act[68] as well as laws discussed above that are concerned with the designation of U.S.-made merchandise, including the Textile Products Identification Act,[69] the Wool Products Labeling Act,[70] and the Fur Products Labeling Act,[71] while prosecuting false "Made-in-U.S.A." designations as to other merchandise through its FTC Act authority.[72] In addition to designations of origin, these laws seek to ensure that consumer commodities are labeled to disclose net contents, identity of commodity, and name and place of business of the product's manufacturer, packer, or distributor.[73]

---

[60]   15 U.S.C. §§ 1601-1667f.

[61]   15 U.S.C. 1666-1666j.

[62]   15 U.S.C. §§ 1681-1681(u).

[63]   15 U.S.C. §§ 1691-1691f.

[64]   15 U.S.C. §§ 1692-1692o.

[65]   15 U.S.C. §§ 1667-1667f.

[66]   15 U.S.C. §§ 1693-1693r.

[67]   15 U.S.C. §§ 2301-2312.

[68]   80 Stat. 1296, 15 U.S.C. §§ 1451-1461.

[69]   15 U.S.C. § 70.

[70]   15 U.S.C. § 68.

[71]   15 U.S.C. § 69.

[72]   *See* FTC Enforcement Policy Statement on U.S. Origin Claims, 62 Fed. Reg. 63756-01 (Dec. 2, 1997), *available at* WL 737641 (F.R.).

[73]   15 U.S.C. § 1453.

c.   FTC Rules, Position Papers, and Guides

The FTC is a prolific issuer of reports, guidelines, advisory, and policy statements.   These materials are widely regarded as useful and well thought out. With the advent of the Internet and, in particular, the FTC's extensive website at http://www.ftc.gov, the FTC's statements and other pronouncements are almost effortlessly available, and are frequently the most convenient authoritative source on an area of law within the FTC's purview.   However, the FTC guides do have limitations.

First, and most importantly, not all of them have been endorsed by courts. Practitioners should be aware that the FTC approaches consumer protection law from a prosecutorial point of view, and the Commission's enforcement intentions are not necessarily the law. On the other hand, knowing the FTC's enforcement intentions can be important in itself. Many firms desire to avoid the risk and expense associated with an FTC investigation and possible litigation.

Second, the FTC's guidelines and policy statements address only the FTC Act and other statutes that the FTC is charged with enforcing, and do not provide guidance to other relevant law.   Many commercial practices within the FTC's ambit are subject to specific regulation at federal, state, and/or local levels, or are the subject of well-developed case law regarding private rights of action. FTC guides are thus best seen as a first step in the investigation of a topic – although, where one is available that relates to the practice of interest, they are often the best first step.   As discussed below, the FTC's reports, guidelines, and pronouncements are frequently employed to interpret the provisions of state consumer protection laws, often at the explicit direction of a state statutory provision or judicial authority.

The major categories of FTC pronouncements described below, in order of authoritativeness, are all compiled and published in the *Code of Federal Regulations*, Volume 16, as updated annually and supplemented daily by the *Federal Register*.

(1) FTC Trade Regulation Rules

The FTC periodically issues Trade Regulation Rules (TRRs) defining unfair or deceptive practices on specific topics.   These are issued only following extensive, albeit informal, hearings, and are considered definitive statements of unfair or deceptive practices under the FTC Act. Under Section 18 of the FTC Act,[74] the Commission is authorized to prescribe "rules which define with specificity acts or

---

[74]   15 U.S.C. § 57a.

practices which are unfair or deceptive acts or practices in or affecting commerce" under Section 5(a)(1) of the Act. Some of the topics on which TRRs have been issued include Credit Practices,[75] Used Cars,[76] Mail Order Merchandise,[77] The Use of Negative Option Plans,[78] Franchising and Business Opportunity Ventures,[79] and Children's Online Privacy.[80]

TRRs provide detailed explanations of deceptive practices that have been identified by the Commission as being of special concern, and often lay out affirmative measures that businesses should take to comply. The FTC Act confers upon the Commission special powers to enforce violations of the Act that contravene a TRR. The FTC may go into federal district court immediately upon a violation "with actual knowledge or knowledge fairly implied on the basis of objective circumstances" to seek civil penalties and up to $11,000 per violation in restitution.[81] In addition, any person who violates a rule (irrespective of the state of knowledge) is liable for injury caused to consumers by the rule violation. The Commission may pursue such recovery in a suit for consumer redress under Section 19 of the FTC Act, 15 U.S.C. Sec. 57b.

Before commencing a rulemaking proceeding the Commission must also have reason to believe that the practices to be addressed by the rulemaking are "prevalent."[82] The chief advantage of establishing a TRR for a given practice is that, where deceptive practices have typical common features, the presence of the TRR eliminates the need to establish in each case whether a defendant has committed a deceptive practice. The FTC accordingly considers whether the advantage of a TRR in efficiently prosecuting deceptive practices outweighs the cost of the rulemaking proceeding. In 2003, for example, the FTC declined to initiate such a proceeding with respect to unsolicited bulk electronic mails ("spam"), in part because spam serves as a vessel for such varying deceptive practices that a concise TRR could not define them with sufficient specificity to make FTC actions more efficient.[83]

---

[75]   16 C.F.R. § 444.
[76]   16 C.F.R. § 455.
[77]   16 C.F.R. § 435.
[78]   16 C.F.R. § 425.
[79]   16 C.F.R. § 436.
[80]   16 C.F.R. § 312.
[81]   15 U.S.C. § 45(m)(1)(A).
[82]   15 U.S.C. § 57a(b)(3).
[83]   FTC Letter, 774 Trade Reg. Rep. (CCH) ¶ 15,363. Not stated in the FTC's reasoning, but likely to have influenced its decision, is the principle that spam per se is not necessarily a deceptive practice, and is entitled to some degree of Constitutional protection. For this reason, the

(2) FTC Guides

FTC Guides to unfair or deceptive practices are issued without the formal proceedings that accompany TRRs. Guides are advisory opinions written by the Commission, and do not carry the special legal presumptions or FTC enforcement powers associated with TRRs. Primarily, they communicate the Commission's views and enforcement intentions with respect to particular areas. Among the topics of FTC Guides are Deceptive Pricing,[84] Debt Collection,[85] and Guarantees.[86]

(3) Other FTC Statements

The FTC issues a variety of other communications relating to unfair and deceptive practices and to its own enforcement intentions. Companies may request and receive FTC advisory opinions on practices they are contemplating, and these opinions are published.[87] Indeed, the Commission rules of practice require that the FTC respond to such requests where a substantial or novel question is raised or if the matter involves a substantial public interest. [88]

Public information campaigns by the FTC address a variety of topics and are directed at different constituencies, including consumers, businesses, and legislators. The Internet has created a new and useful venue for such campaigns. Recently, for example, the FTC launched a new Internet site dedicated to "consumer information security," aimed primarily at consumers.[89] Featuring the mascot Dewie the Turtle, the FTC's site includes pages and activities designed for younger consumers as well as information on FTC privacy protection policies and enforcement efforts for adult consumers and businesses.

B.   Private Actions under the Lanham Act

The Lanham Act is, first and foremost, a trademark statute. The Act was preceded by the Trademark Act of 1920, which for the first time established a limited federal private right of action for false representations made in advertising as to the geographic origin of a product. The Lanham Act – formally titled the Federal Trademark Act of 1946 – repealed these provisions and broadened the right of action to

---

FTC reserves its attacks on spam for cases in which spam is used to promote practices meeting traditional definitions of deception.

[84]   16 C.F.R. § 233.
[85]   16 C.F.R. § 237.
[86]   16 C.F.R. § 239.
[87]   16 C.F.R. § 1.1(a).
[88]   16 C.F.R. § 1.1(a)(1)-(2).
[89]   *See* http://www.ftc.gov/infosecurity.

include other trademark- and trade-dress-related claims, such as the "passing off" of one's goods or services as those of another, or misrepresentations relating to the sponsorship or approval of the goods or services by another party.[90] In Section 43(a), however, the Lanham Act also prohibited "any false description or representation...tending falsely to describe or represent the [goods or services]."[91] Any false description or representation about the goods or service that entered interstate commerce is now actionable.

Section 43(a)'s broadening of the trademark right of action was radical, and fit rather uneasily in a trademark statute. As we have seen, false representations about features of products other than those causing consumer confusion about where they came from have traditionally been regarded as deceptive practices injuring mainly consumers. However, the broad scope of this language was amply reaffirmed in two separate rewritings of Section 43(a), in 1988[92] and 1992.[93] Currently, Section 43(a)(1)(B) prohibits "any false or misleading description of fact, or false or misleading representation of fact, which ... misrepresents the *nature, characteristics, qualities*, or geographic origin of his or her or another person's goods, services, or commercial activities."[94] These amendments also broadened the right of action still further by adding false and misleading statements about another's products or services (*i.e.,* disparagement) to the catalog of unlawful acts.

The Lanham Act provides that "[a]ny person who, on or in connection with any goods or services, or any container for goods, uses in commerce" any false or misleading description of fact (*inter alia*) shall be liable.[95] Most often, the "person" in question is the company providing the product or service being advertised. However, additional parties with an interest in the advertising may also be liable. Thus, an advertising agency is sometimes sued under the Lanham Act together with its client,[96] and in at least one case was initially found jointly and

---

[90]   15 U.S.C. § 1125(a).

[91]   *Id.*

[92]   Trademark Law Revision Act of 1988, Pub. L. No. 100-667, 102 Stat. 3935 (effective November 16, 1989) (codified as amended at 15 U.S.C. § 1125(a)).

[93]   Trademark Law Clarification Act, Pub. L. 102-542, 106 Stat. 3568 (1992) (codified at 15 U.S.C. § 1125(a)).

[94]   15 U.S.C. § 1125(a)(1)(B) (emphasis added).

[95]   15 U.S.C. § 1125(a).

[96]   *See, e.g.,* Am. Home Prods. Corp. v. Johnson & Johnson, 654 F. Supp. 568 (S.D.N.Y. 1987); Am. Brands, Inc. v. R. J. Reynolds Tobacco Co., 413 F. Supp. 1352 (S.D.N.Y. 1976); Proctor & Gamble Co. v.

severally liable where it participated actively in the creation, development, and propagation of the false advertisements.[97] Individuals affiliated with the company whose product or service is advertised may also be held liable, but again, they must be personally involved in the creation or dissemination of the advertisement at issue.[98]

1. Elements of a Claim

The general elements of a Lanham Act violation are:
1. the defendant made a statement about its own or a competitor's product;
2. the defendant's statement was false or misleading, and actually deceived or had the tendency to deceive a substantial segment of its intended audience;
3. the statement was made in connection with commercial advertising or promotion;
4. the deception was material; and
5. the false advertising causes injury to the plaintiff.[99]

a. Statement

As discussed above,[100] only affirmative statements, as opposed to omissions, are generally actionable under the Lanham Act. Omissions come into play inasmuch as an affirmative statement may be false or misleading if it is incomplete or if additional qualifications, exceptions, or conditions, or other facts are not stated at the same time.

b. False or Misleading Nature of Statement

The plaintiff in a Lanham Act case must allege and, if the meaning of the statement is not facially clear, prove that a particular statement

---

[97] Chesebrough-Ponds, Inc., 747 F.2d 114 (2d Cir. 1984); Tambrands, Inc. v. Warner-Lambert Co., 673 F. Supp. 1190 (S.D.N.Y. 1987).
Gillette Co. v. Wilkinson Sword, Inc., No. 89 CV 3586 (KMW), 1992 WL 30938 (S.D.N.Y. Feb. 3, 1992), *modified*, 795 F. Supp. 662 (S.D.N.Y. 1992), *vacated in part*, 1992 WL 12000396 (Oct. 28, 1992).

[98] *See* Nat'l Survival Game, Inc. v. Skirmish U.S.A., Inc., 603 F. Supp. 339, 341 (S.D.N.Y. 1985).

[99] *See* Johnson & Johnson-Merck Consumer Pharm. Co. v. Rhone-Poulenc Rorer Pharm., Inc., 19 F.3d 125, 129 (3d Cir. 1994).

[100] *See supra* 1.B.2.

was made. The plaintiff must then prove that this statement is false or misleading.[101]

The general process of determining the meaning of a challenged statement has been described above.[102] In the case of an express claim, the plaintiff bases its allegation of falsity on the literal meaning of the words or depictions used in the advertisement.[103] In some circuits, courts also recognize that literal falsity may flow from necessary implications of the words or depictions – meanings that, while not literally stated in the advertisement, will inevitably be understood.[104] In theory, the literal meaning of an express claim should be self-evident, although in practice the vagaries of the English language often leave something to litigate. If the plaintiff alleges (or the defendant successfully argues) that the claim is implied, then the plaintiff must prove that consumers infer the alleged statement from the advertisement. In some cases an expert on consumer perception can testify effectively as to the implied meaning of an advertisement, but more generally a consumer survey is used.[105]

Like any evidence, the consumer survey is fair game for attack by the defendant. The defendant may mount a critique of the plaintiff's survey and/or may introduce a survey of its own, which will be subject to attack by the plaintiff. There is considerable jurisprudence on methodological features of surveys that constitute strengths or flaws.[106]

---

[101]   *See* Skil Corp. v. Rockwell Int'l Corp., 375 F. Supp. 777, 782-83 (N.D. Ill. 1974).

[102]   *See supra* 1.B.1-2.

[103]   An example of a literally false nonverbal depiction is the use by a defendant of a photograph of another's product in its advertising, in a context that makes it clear that the photograph is intended to depict the defendant's product. *See*, e.g., L'Aiglon Apparel, Inc. v. Lana Lobell, Inc., 214 F.2d 649 (3d Cir. 1954).

[104]   *See* Novartis Consumer Health, Inc. v. Johnson & Johnson-Merck Pharms. Co., 290 F.3d 578, 586-87 (3d Cir. 2002); Pharmacia Corp. v. GlaxoSmithKline Consumer Healthcare, L.P., 292 F. Supp. 2d 611, 614 (D.N.J. 2003).

[105]   *See*, e.g., McNeilab, Inc. v. American Home Prods. Corp., 501 F. Supp. 517, 528 (S.D.N.Y.), *modified on other grounds*, 501 F. Supp. 540 (S.D.N.Y. 1980).

[106]   *See*, e.g., Am. Home Prods. v. Proctor & Gamble, 871 F. Supp. 739, 761 (D.N.J. 1994) (criticizing unrealistic presentation of advertisement to research subjects and lack of controls and filter questions); Johnson & Johnson-Merck Consumer Pharm. Co. v. Smithkline Beecham Corp., 960 F.2d 294, 300 (2d Cir. 1992) (criticizing leading questions); Johnson & Johnson-Merck Consumer Pharm. Co. v. Rhone-Poulenc Rorer Pharm., Inc., 19 F.3d 125, 135-36 (3d Cir. 1994) (same); Hertz Corp. v. Avis,

Because the conclusions of courts may not necessarily coincide with academic standards, it is essential to review the Lanham Act case law, especially in the relevant circuit and district, for guidance before arranging for a consumer survey.

Once the meaning of the statement is established, the plaintiff must prove that the statement is false or misleading. This, too, can be virtually automatic or it can involve lengthy litigation and extrinsic evidence. Where the claim involves the effectiveness or performance of either the defendant's product or a competing product, the plaintiff must prove, often through expert testimony or appropriate scientific tests, that the product does not perform as stated.[107] Where the statement is that the defendant's product is superior to its competitor's in some respect, the plaintiff must introduce evidence that the defendant's product is actually equivalent or inferior.[108] As with evidence of the statement's meaning, the defendant may introduce counter-evidence, sparking a battle of experts or of research studies.[109]

One further alternative in proving that an advertisement implies a false claim is evidence of the defendant's subjective intent. Although the defendant's state of mind nominally plays no role in establishing Lanham Act liability, intent to deceive has been held to obviate the need for extrinsic evidence that the advertisement carries a misleading implication.[110]

Generally, merely unsubstantiated advertising is not actionable under the Lanham Act.[111] In recent years, some courts have begun to recognize that, where the advertiser's claim is completely devoid of credible substantiation, a statement may be so groundless as to be deemed false without the need for plaintiffs to provide evidence of its falsity,[112]

Inc., 867 F. Supp. 208, 213 (S.D.N.Y. 1994) (criticizing closed-ended question as leading).

[107] *See* Castrol, Inc. v. Quaker State Corp., 977 F.2d 57, 63 (2d Cir. 1992).

[108] *See* Toro Co. v. Textron, Inc., 499 F. Supp. 241 (D. Del. 1980) (finding against plaintiff that failed to show that its product performed as well as defendant's product, for which superiority was claimed).

[109] One party can sometimes meet its burden without introducing new evidence by reinterpreting the other party's results. *See, e.g.*, Accu-Sort Sys., Inc., v. Lazardata Corp., 820 F. Supp. 928, 932 n.7 (E.D. Pa. 1993); McNeil-P.C.C., Inc. v. Bristol-Myers Squibb Co., 938 F.2d 1544, 1546-49 (2d Cir. 1991)

[110] *Johnson & Johnson-Merck*, 960 F.2d at 298-99.

[111] *See* Procter & Gamble Co. v. Chesebrough-Pond's Inc., 747 F.2d 114, 119 (2d Cir. 1984).

[112] *See, e.g.*, Sandoz Pharm. Corp. v. Richardson-Vicks, Inc., 902 F.2d 222, 228 n.7; *Pharmacia*, 292 F. Supp. 2d at 621; *Accu-Sort Sys.*, 820 F. Supp. at 932 n.7.

Special rules for two types of claim discussed above as general advertising principles should be noted again here. First, *establishment claims* that "explicitly or implicitly represent[] that tests or studies prove its product superior" – *e.g.*, "tests prove that product X works" – are interpreted as claims that the evidence exists and meets prevailing standards of validity, not just that the underlying claim is true.[113] Second, *puffing* – statements that because of obvious hyperbole, vagueness, or opinion cannot be said to be "aspecific and measurable claim, capable of being proved false" – are generally not subject to Lanham Act attack.[114]

Those wishing to challenge a competitor's unsubstantiated advertising have a further alternative under certain circumstances, although it is not strictly a form of legal action. Where the advertising complained of is "national" – that is, disseminated on a "nationwide or broadly regional basis" through media such as television, radio, magazines, newspapers, the Internet, or direct mail – anyone may lodge a complaint with the National Advertising Division (NAD) of the Council of Better Business Bureaus.[115] NAD is an advertising industry self-regulatory body that reviews advertising under its own set of procedures, using standards for truthful advertising generally similar to those of the FTC. These standards include the requirement that advertising be substantiated. While the NAD review process culminates in recommendations that are not legally binding, the NAD may refer instances of failure to follow its recommendations to the FTC, which is generally respectful of the NAD's findings and may launch an investigation.

c. Commercial Advertising or Promotion

Section 43(a)(1)(B) limits liability for false or misleading statements to "commercial advertising and promotion."[116] This encompasses essentially any communication with a public audience where the purpose

---

[113] *See supra* 1.B.6. *See also* Castrol, Inc. v. Quaker State Corp., 977 F.2d 57, 63 (2d Cir. 1992); Proctor & Gamble Co. v. Cheesbrough Pond's Inc., 747 F.2d at 119 (2d Cir. 1984); Pfizer, Inc. v. Miles, Inc., 868 F. Supp. 437, 457 (D. Conn. 1994).

[114] *See* Pizza Hut, Inc. v. Papa John's Int'l, Inc., 227 F.3d 489, 496 (5th Cir. 2000), *cert. denied*, 532 U.S. 920 (2001); *see also supra* 1.B.1; Bose Corp. v. Linear Design Labs, Inc., 467 F.2d 304, 310-11 (2d Cir. 1972); *In re* Century 21-Re/Max Real Estate Advertising Litig., 882 F. Supp. 915, 926 (C.D. Ca. 1994).

[115] *See generally* http://www.nadreview.org.html.

[116] 15 U.S.C. § 1125(a)(1)(B).

is promotion of the product, including packaging and labeling,[117] literature accompanying free samples,[118] press releases,[119] and customer telephone solicitations.[120] Communications with private, nonconsumer audiences cannot give rise to a Lanham Act suit,[121] nor can communications whose purpose is not to influence customers to purchase the product or service, such as statements to shareholders.[122] However, some communications that do not appear to come within the scope of product or service promotion have been held by some courts to be a basis of liability, so the Lanham Act case law of a particular type of communication should be researched where there is any question.[123]

d. Materiality

A statement is material under the Lanham Act if it is likely to influence purchasing decisions.[124] In practice, this is not a difficult burden to meet. Representations that are literally false (as opposed to conveying a false implication) are presumed to be material.[125] In order to be found not material, the subject of a representation must be "trivial."[126]

---

117   *See, e.g.,* PPX Enters., Inc. v. Audiofidelity Enters., Inc., 818 F.2d 266, 272 (2d Cir. 1987) (depiction of performer on musical recording packaging).

118   *See* Mylan Labs, Inc. v. Pharm. Basics, Inc., 808 F. Supp. 446, 458 (D. Md. 1992), *rev'd in part on other grounds sub nom. Mylan Labs, Inc. v. Matkari,* 7 F.3d 1130 (4th Cir. 1993), *cert denied sub nom.* Am. Home Prods. Corp. v. Mylan Labs., Inc., 510 U.S. 1997 (1994).

119   *See, e.g.,* Truck Components, Inc. v. K-H Corp., 776 F. Supp. 405, 407-08 (N.D. Ill. 1991).

120   National Artists Mgmt. Co. v. Weaving, 769 F. Supp. 1224, 1230 (S.D.N.Y. 1991).

121   *See* Eventmedia Int'l, Inc. v. Time Inc. Magazine Co., 1992-2 Trade Cas. (CCH) ¶ 70,029, at 69,055 (S.D.N.Y. 1992).

122   *See* Musicom Int'l, Inc. v. Serubo, Civ. A. No. 94-1920, 1994 WL 105551 (E.D. Pa. Mar. 29, 1994).

123   *See, e.g.,* Towers Fin. Corp. v. Dun & Bradstreet, Inc., 803 F. Supp. 820, 824 (S.D.N.Y. 1991) (finding Dun & Bradstreet business information reports advertising or promotion); *compare* Gordon & Breach Science Publishers S.A. v. Am. Inst. of Physics, 859 F. Supp. 1521, 1544 (S.D.N.Y. 1994) (finding criticism of competitor's product in trade journal may be actionable) *with* Semco, Inc. v. Amcast, Inc., 52 F.3d 108 (6th Cir. 1995) (finding criticism of competitor's product in scientific journal not actionable).

124   U.S. Healthcare, Inc. v. Blue Cross of Greater Phila., 898 F.2d 914, 922 (3d Cir.), *cert. denied,* 498 U.S. 816 (1990).

125   *See* Alpo Petfoods, Inc. v. Ralston Purina Co., 720 F. Supp. 194, 213 (D.D.C. 1989), *aff'd in part, rev'd in part on other grounds,* 913 F.2d 958

e. Injury

To obtain injunctive relief, a Lanham Act plaintiff must show that it has a reasonable basis to believe that it is likely to suffer some injury relating to the false or misleading nature of the challenged advertisement.[127] The plaintiff need not show that the amount of injury will be substantial or that any actual injury has already occurred, unless monetary damages (see below) are sought. Injury is presumed when a comparative advertisement mentioning the plaintiff's product has been found to be false.[128]

2. Standing

The Lanham Act provides that anyone committing a Section 43(a)(1) violation "shall be liable in a civil action by any person who believes that he or she is likely to be damaged by such act,"[129] but it is well settled that the Lanham Act was intended to, and does, provide a remedy only for competitors and others who have been damaged not by the defendant's false representations as such, but by the commercial advantage gained from making them.[130] This reflects the Act's primary orientation as the

---

(D.C. Cir. 1990), *order modified*, 1991 WL 25793 (D.D.C. 1991), *aff'd in part, modified in part, rev'd in part on other grounds*, 997 F.2d 949 (D.C. Cir. 1993).

[126] *See, e.g.,* Borden, Inc. v. Kraft, Inc., 224 U.S.P.Q. 811, 819 (N.D. Ill. 1984) (finding difference between 4.6-oz and 5-oz. Package size trivial).

[127] *See* Johnson & Johnson v. Carter-Wallace Inc., 631 F.2d 186, 190-91 (2d Cir. 1980).

[128] *See* Novartis Consumer Health, Inc. v. Johnson & Johnson-Merck Consumer Pharm. Co., 129 F. Supp. 2d 351, 367 (D.N.J. 2000), *aff'd*, 290 F.3d 578, 586-87 (3d Cir. 2002).

[129] 15 U.S.C. § 1125(a)(1).

[130] *See* Colligan v. Activities Club of New York, Ltd., 442 F.2d 686, 692 (2d Cir.) ("The Act's purpose...is exclusively to protect the interests of 'a purely commercial class against unscrupulous commercial conduct.'") (citations omitted), *cert. denied*, 404 U.S. 1004 (1971); *see also* FTC v. Brown & Williamson Tobacco Corp., 778 F.2d 35, 40 (D.C. Cir. 1985) ("The Lanham Act does constitute a private remedial scheme for the benefit of disgruntled competitors whereas the FTC Act more specifically serves the public interest and is enforced by the FTC."). Under certain theories related to false advertising, plaintiffs may have Lanham Act standing based on other types of commercial harm. For example, a celebrity whose voice has been imitated in a commercial without disclosure may have a claim for "false endorsement" under the Lanham Act, although this type of claim is a form of "misuse of trademark" and

federal trademark statute, providing a right of action for trademark and trade dress infringement – where competitors are generally the primary party injured – and, at least originally, only incidentally for general false advertising, where competitors can be injured as well as consumers.

At the margin, what constitutes a competitor has been the subject of some debate and litigation. Courts do not expend resources on a full-fledged, antitrust-style market definition analysis to determine whether the plaintiff and defendant in a Lanham Act case compete in the same product market. If products are plausibly seen by some consumers as substitutable or even as associated in use, this can suffice to establish the necessary relationship.[131]

Whether a *prospective or potential* competitor has standing to make a Lanham Act challenge is less clear. The outcome may depend on how likely and imminent the introduction of the plaintiff's competing product is. The decided cases, which are split on the issue, deal with pharmaceutical companies, which must apply with the FDA before marketing a new product and thus display a clear intention to do so.[132] Plaintiffs that cannot produce such clear evidence that they intend to market a competing product may face a more difficult hurdle.

It is well established that a trade association may sue under the Lanham Act on behalf of either its individual members or itself.[133] The basis for this standing has generally been that the trade association has an interest in the sales of its member companies, either directly because dues to the trade association may be tied to sales levels, or indirectly

---

not strictly false advertising. *See* Waits v. Frito-Lay, Inc., 978 F.2d 1093 (9th Cir. 1992), *cert. denied*, 506 U.S. 1080 (1993).

[131] *See, e.g.,* Johnson & Johnson v. Carter-Wallace, Inc., 631 F.2d 186, 190 (2d Cir. 1980) (finding maker of body lotion a competitor of depilatory manufacturer based on applications of both products in hair removal).

[132] *Compare* Upjohn Co. v. Riahom Corp., 641 F. Supp. 1209, 1225 n.18 (D. Del. 1986) (finding pharmaceutical company may recover under Lanham Act prior to gaining FDA approval to market competing product) *with* Ortho Pharm. Corp. v. Cosprophar, Inc., 828 F. Supp. 1114 (S.D.N.Y. 1993) (cost/fees proceeding); 1993 U.S. Dist. LEXIS 15193 (S.D.N.Y. Oct. 28, 1993), *aff'd*, 32 F.3d 690 (2d Cir. 1994) (finding pharmaceutical company may not recover under Lanham Act prior to gaining FDA approval to market competing product).

[133] *See, e.g.,* Camel Hair & Cashmere Inst. v. Saks Fifth Ave. 284 F.3d 302 (1st Cir.), *cert. denied sub nom.* Saks Fifth Ave. v. Cashmere & Camel Hair Manuf. Inst., 537 U.S. 1001 (2002); Nat'l Ass'n of Pharm. Mfrs., Inc. v. Ayerst Labs., 850 F.2d 904, 914 (2d Cir. 1988); Camel Hair & Cashmere Inst., Inc. v. Associated Dry Goods Corp., 799 F.2d 6 (1st Cir. 1986).

inasmuch as profitable members make for a healthy trade association.[134] Similarly, other entities with clear financial interests in an entity that competes with the advertiser have been granted standing.[135] However, as the would-be plaintiff moves further from being a direct competitor, standing becomes less certain. For example, retailers of products that compete with an advertiser's products have been held not to have Lanham Act standing to sue that manufacturer for false advertising.[136]

In researching standing under the Lanham Act, it is risky to rely on precedent derived from the trademark-related provisions of the statute. At least two circuits have ruled that standing under Section 43(a) is more narrowly limited to parties having a competitive relationship with the defendant than under the Act's other provisions.[137] What is certain is that consumers do not have standing.[138]

Class actions under the Lanham Act are rare, but they do occur and there are no special barriers to pursuing them. The lack of a right of action for consumers removes the most obvious potential audience for Lanham Act class actions. A group of competitors seeking to pursue a class action under the Lanham Act would often have difficulty under the class certification standard of Federal Rule 23, because each putative class member would likely have unique, individualized facts determining both the existence of injury and the amount of damages.[139]

---

[134] *See* Potato Chip Inst. v. General Mills, Inc., 333 F. Supp. 173, 179 (D. Neb. 1971), *aff'd*, 461 F.2d 1088 (8th Cir. 1972) (conferring standing on trade association in part because a substantial portion of its income was derived from dues of member firms, which were linked to member firms' sales).

[135] *See, e.g.*, Thorn v. Reliance Van Co., 736 F.2d 929 (3d Cir. 1984) (director and 45% shareholder of bankrupt concern have standing); PPX Enters., Inc. v. Audiofidelity Enters., Inc., 818 F.2d 266, 268 (2d Cir. 1987) (licensee of intellectual property relevant to false advertising).

[136] *See* Conte Bros. Auto., Inc. v. Quaker State-Slick 50, Inc., 165 F.3d 221, 223 (3d Cir. 1998).

[137] *See* Waits v. Frito-Lay, Inc., 978 F.2d 1093, 1110 (9th Cir. 1992), *cert. denied*, 506 U.S. 1080 (1993); Stanfield v. Osborne Indus., Inc., 52 F.3d 867, 873 (10th Cir.), *cert. denied*, 516 U.S. 920 (1995).

[138] *See, e.g.*, Colligan v. Activities Club of New York, Ltd., 442 F.2d 686 (2d Cir.), *cert. denied*, 404 U.S. 1004 (1971); Serbin v. Ziebart Int'l Corp., 11 F.3d 1163 (3d Cir. 1993); Barrus v. Sylvania, 55 F.3d 468, 469 (9th Cir. 1995).

[139] FED. R. CIV. P. 23(b) (class action maintainable only if "the court finds that the questions of law or fact common to the members of the class predominate over any questions affecting only individual members").

3. *Remedies*

a. Injunctive Relief

Competitors often act quickly when someone begins disseminating an advertisement that they consider objectionable. In a competitive industry, companies often monitor their rivals advertising closely. As described below, the monetary damages to competitors that can stem from a deceptive advertising campaign can be difficult to assess or calculate, and in many instances relief from the courts comes as too little, too late. Market share may be irretrievably lost, affecting financial performance for the indefinite future. Because of these factors, injunctive relief is frequently the Lanham Act plaintiff's main priority, and many Lanham Act cases are effectively ended at the preliminary injunction stage. If the plaintiff's motion for a preliminary injunction is granted, the case often settles quickly because the plaintiff has what it wants and the defendant has little incentive to defend an advertising campaign that has effectively been killed. If the motion is denied, the plaintiff faces the prospect of litigating advertisements that will likely have done their damage long before the merits are decided, and usually with adverse statements already voiced by the court in the injunction opinion as to the ultimate outcome. Nevertheless, a significant number of Lanham Act plaintiffs do pursue monetary damages, as described below.

Injunctive relief under the Lanham Act is provided under Section 34(a) of the Act and applies equally to violations of the trademark-related and deceptive advertising provisions of the Act.[140] Plaintiffs and counterclaim plaintiffs may seek temporary restraining orders, preliminary injunctions, and permanent junctions under the standards that prevail in the federal circuit where the case is brought.[141]

Other equitable relief is also available to the court. This can include remedial packaging and corrective advertising containing court-

---

[140]   15 U.S.C. § 1116(a).

[141]   The most commonly litigated form of injunctive Lanham Act relief is the preliminary injunction. For examples of the preliminary judgment standard as applied to advertising in various circuits, *see* Johnson & Johnson v. Carter-Wallace, Inc., 631 F.2d 186, 189 (2d Cir. 1980); Johnson & Johnson-Merck Consumer Pharm. Co. v. Rhone-Poulenc Rorer Pharm., Inc., Civ. A. No. 91-7099, 1993 WL 21239, at *7 (E.D. Pa. Jan. 29, 1993), *aff'd*, 19 F.3d 125 (3d Cir. 1994); Honeywell, Inc. v. Control Solutions, Inc., 1994-2 Trade Cas. (CCH) ¶ 70,828 (N.D. Ohio 1994) (citing Sixth Circuit standard).

mandated statements or disclaimers to attempt to correct false impressions in the marketplace.[142]

b.   Monetary Damages

To recover monetary damages, the plaintiff must prove an additional element as part of its claim: that the challenged advertisement not only has the tendency to deceive consumers (*i.e.* was false or misleading, as elaborated above), but actually does deceive a significant number of consumers in its intended audience.[143] Developments in the market can furnish such evidence, in cases where the defendant's deceptive advertising is so effective that it causes substantial competitive gains against plaintiff's product.[144]

The monetary remedies to which successful Lanham Act plaintiffs and counterclaim plaintiffs are entitled are provided by Section 35(a) of the Act.[145] As provided in that section, the plaintiff may recover "(1) defendant's profits, (2) any damages sustained by the plaintiff, and (3) the costs of the action."[146] Although all three types of damages are named in the statute, not all are awarded as a matter of course.

---

[142]   *See, e.g.,* Upjohn v. Riahom Corp., 641 F. Supp. 1209, 1226 (D. Del. 1986) (ordering corrective packaging); Potato Chip Inst. v. General Mills, Inc., 333 F. Supp. 173 (D. Neb. 1971), *aff'd,* 461 F.2d 1088 (8th Cir. 1972) (same); Alpo Petfoods, Inc. v. Ralston Purina Co., 720 F. Supp. 194, 216 (D.D.C. 1989), *aff'd in part, rev'd in part on other grounds,* 913 F.2d 958 (D.C. Cir. 1990), *order modified,* 1991 WL 25793 (D.D.C. 1991), *aff'd in part, modified in part, rev'd in part on other grounds,* 997 F.2d 949 (D.C. Cir. 1993) (ordering corrective advertising); Thomas Nelson, Inc. v. Cherish Books Ltd., 595 F. Supp. 989 (S.D.N.Y. 1984) (same).

[143]   *See* Hesmer Foods, Inc. v. Cambell Soup Co., 346 F.2d 356, 359 (7th Cir.), *cert. denied,* 382 U.S. 839 (1965); U-Haul Int'l Inc. v. Jartran, Inc., 601 F. Supp. 1140, 1149 (D. Ariz. 1984), *aff'd,* 793 F.2d 1034 (9th Cir. 1986).

[144]   *See, e.g.,* Gillette Co. v. Wilkinson Sword, Inc., No. 89 CV 3586 (KMW), 1992 WL 30938, at *2 (S.D.N.Y. Feb. 3, 1992), *modified,* 795 F. Supp. 662 (S.D.N.Y. 1992), *vacated in part,* 1992 WL 12000396 (Oct. 28, 1992). However, courts differ in the extent to which they will credit such evidence when other factors are cited that may explain the market developments. *See, e.g.,* Tambrands, Inc. v. Warner-Lambert Co., 673 F. Supp. 1190, 1197-98 (S.D.N.Y. 1987) (rejecting damages claim because other forces may have caused market share decline); BASF Corp. v. Old World Trading Co., 41 F.3d 1081, 1086-87 (7th Cir. 1994) (recalculating lost profits damages to account for effect of other market factors).

[145]   15 U.S.C. § 1117(a).

[146]   15 U.S.C. §§ 1117(a)(1)-1117(a)(3).

(1) Plaintiff's Lost Profits

The primary measure of the plaintiff's damages is its lost profits, both from sales lost to the defendant as a result of the challenged advertising and from any price reductions necessary to compete in the face of the defendant's false advertisements.[147] The plaintiff's damages may also include its costs to fund a corrective advertising campaign to address the misperceptions created by the deceptive advertising in the minds of consumers, and incidental elements such as loss of goodwill.[148] Proof of these damages often will be imprecise. Plaintiffs are supposed to allege monetary damages with specificity, but courts will often engage in some extrapolation to arrive at a final figure.[149] Moreover, when courts award damages, they typically set an amount and cite several contributing factors without apportioning share of harm among them.[150] Thus, the contribution of each factor often is unclear.

The Lanham Act provides that the court may award up to treble the actual proven damages, but this is neither required nor necessarily intended to be punitive.[151] It may reflect the difficulty of proving the amount of monetary damages and reflects the likelihood that the plaintiff has been injured to a greater extent than it can prove.[152] For this reason, courts are more likely to enhance damages in the presence of factors suggesting that the plaintiff's proven damages are underestimated. Examples of this are severe market distortions and heavy competitive expenditures undertaken by the plaintiff as a result of the challenged advertising.[153] With extended damages, amounts as high as $40 million have been awarded in Lanham Act cases.[154]

---

[147] 15 U.S.C. § 1117(a)(1).

[148] *See* Mobius Mgmt. Sys., Inc. v. Fourth Dimension Software, Inc., 880 F. Supp. 1005, 1023 (S.D.N.Y. 1994) (awarding cost of corrective marketing efforts); U-Haul Int'l, Inc. v. Jartran, Inc., 793 F.2d 1034, 1041 (9th Cir. 1986) (awarding cost of retaliatory advertising).

[149] *See* PPX Enters., Inc. v. Audiofidelity Enters., Inc., 818 F.2d 266, 271 (2d Cir. 1987).

[150] *See, e.g., U-Haul Int'l.*, 793 F.3d 1034.

[151] 15 U.S.C. § 1117(a).

[152] *See, e.g., Mobius Mgmt Sys., Inc.*, 880 F. Supp. at 1025-26.

[153] *See, e.g.,* Alpo Petfoods, Inc. v. Ralston Purina Co., 778 F. Supp. 555, 564 (D.D.C.), *order amended by* No. CIV.A. 86-2728(SS), 1991 WL 1292963 (D.D.C. 1991), *aff'd in part, rev'd in part on other grounds,* 997 F.2d 949 (D.C. Cir. 1993).

[154] *See* U-Haul Int'l, Inc. v. Jartran, Inc., 601 F. Supp. 1140 (D. Ariz. 1984), *aff'd,* 793 F.2d 1034 (9th Cir. 1986) (awarding $40 million after doubling).

(2) Defendant's Profits

In some circuits, the successful plaintiff can recover the defendant's profits only upon a showing that the defendant acted with intent to deceive.[155] Other theories for determining when a plaintiff deserves defendant's profits arising from the deception are cases where the defendant is unjustly enriched or where the defendant's conduct suggests that an extra assessment is necessary to deter future transgressions.[156]

(3) Costs

Recovery of costs is authorized by the Act only in "exceptional cases."[157] The plaintiff's costs of litigation – chiefly its attorneys' fees – are generally available only in especially egregious cases of intentional deception.[158] The defendant's conduct must usually exceed the willfulness required in some circuits for the plaintiff to recover defendant's profits; it must rise to the level of maliciousness and fraud.[159]

4. Counterclaims

Counterclaims are common in Lanham Act suits. As mentioned above, firms in competitive markets often continually monitor each other's advertising, frequently with a jaundiced eye. When an advertising challenge is made, either in the form of a demand letter or Lanham Act complaint, the target frequently responds with its own accusations and claims.[160] These may involve the original challenger's advertising for its competing product or, if the firms compete in multiple product categories, separate products. Under Fed. R. Civ. Pro. 13(b), the

---

[155] George Basch Co. v. Blue Coral, Inc., 968 F.2d 1532, 1534, 1540 (2d Cir.), *cert. denied*, 506 U.S. 991 (1992); Texas Pig Stands, Inc. v. Hard Rock Café Int'l Inc., 951 F.2d 684 (5th Cir. 1992); BASF Corp. v. Old World Trading Co., 41 F.3d 1081, 1086-87 (7th Cir. 1996).

[156] *See, e.g., Blue Coral, Inc.* 968 F.2d at 1537; Burndy Corp. v. Teledyne Indus, Inc., 748 F. 2d 767, 772 (2d Cir. 1984).

[157] 15 U.S.C. § 1117(a).

[158] Alpo Pet Foods, Inc. v. Ralston Purina Co., 913 F.2d 958 (D.C. Cir. 1990), *order modified*, 1991 WL 25793 (D.D.C. Feb. 8, 1991), *reh'g to recomputed damages*, 778 F. Supp. 555 (D.D.C. 1991), *aff'd in part, modified in part, rev'd in part*, 997 F.2d 949 (D.C. Cir. 1993); Mobius Mgm.t Sys., Inc. v. Fourth Dimension Software, Inc., 880 F. Supp. 1005 (S.D.N.Y. 1994).

[159] *See Mobius Mgmt. Sys., Inc.*, 880 F. Supp. at 1025.

[160] *See, e.g.,* IQ Prods. Co. v. Pennzoil Prods. Co., 305 F.3d 368 (5th Cir. 2002), *cert. denied*, 538 U.S. 944 (2003).

counterclaims can also be unrelated to false advertising and concern any claim between the parties.[161]

Lanham Act cases between competitors sometimes escalate into multi-faceted, drawn-out legal battles. The advertising situation during these Lanham Act battles is usually dynamic. Often, the marketing department is as eager as the legal department to respond to the competitor's challenges. New advertisements may be produced and disseminated by both sides. These, in turn, may provoke amended complaints and still further claims. The resulting conflict on two fronts can become difficult to manage, and the advertisements that spawned the original complaint may, by this time, have become obsolete and been superseded by new advertisements influenced by the litigation.

Counterclaims are such an accepted strategy in Lanham Act litigation that a prospective plaintiff is always well advised to review its own advertising for truthfulness before launching a legal challenge to that of its competitor. Experienced advertising counsel know that the first reaction of a target will be to examine the advertising of the challenger to assess what counterclaims it can mount. The defendant hopes to be able to assert claims that are more serious and imply greater damages than those alleged by the originator of the dispute, and sometimes succeeds.

---

[161]   *See, e.g.,* Sally Beauty Co., Inc. v. Beautyco, Inc., 304 F.3d 964 (10th Cir. 2002) (claim for trademark infringement, trade dress infringement, and false advertising provoked counterclaims for state law antitrust and unfair competition violations).

STATE CONSUMER PROTECTION LAW AND ENFORCEMENT

Governmental units within the United States take seriously their responsibility to protect consumers from unfair and deceptive practices. All states, the District of Columbia, and many local governments have enacted consumer protection laws or unfair and deceptive acts and practices (UDAP) statutes of one form or another. Many of these laws were enacted during and after the wave of consumerism that swept the United States starting in the mid-1960s, making them relatively young laws but old enough to have a substantial history of judicial interpretation. Often, however, reported case law under a given state or local consumer protection law may be quite thin. Not only do states vary greatly in their enforcement aggressiveness, but consumer protection cases are less likely than many others to be litigated through trial. The statutes themselves can also provide little guidance, often being worded as broadly as possible so as to allow the greatest breadth and flexibility of action by enforcement agencies and plaintiffs, and for liberal interpretation by courts to protect consumers.[1]

It would require at least a chapter on each state's consumer protection laws to convey even a general overview. The consumer protection statutes of several of the more active states have been the subjects of entire treatises.[2] For these reasons, a general treatment of state consumer protection laws such as this can provide only a starting point for analysis. This chapter sketches, in the very broadest terms, the areas covered by state consumer protection laws and some of the respects in which these typically differ from federal counterparts. Individual states will provide exceptions to almost every generalization made in the following pages. Lists of states whose UDAP laws possess certain characteristics are provided as examples, but are not exhaustive. No practitioner should undertake to counsel under any state's consumer protection laws without researching state-specific resources, to which this handbook seeks to provide only initial vectors. Review of

---

[1]   *See, e.g.,* Boubelik v. Liberty State Bank, 527 N.W.2d 589, 592 (Minn. App. 1995) *rev'd on other grounds*, 553 N.W.2d 393 (Minn. 1996); Iadanza v. Mather, 820 F. Supp. 1371 (D. Utah 1993); Smith v. Commercial Banking Corp., 866 F.2d 576 (3d Cir. 1989).

[2]   *See, e.g.,* Robert M. Langer et al., CONNECTICUT UNFAIR TRADE PRACTICES, Connecticut Practice Series vol. 12 (2003).

specialized consumer protection and trade regulation reporters and contact with state or local enforcement agencies also are important elements of legal research in this area.

FTC jurisprudence and publications often are a good first starting point for interpreting even those state UDAP statutes that have little facial resemblance to the FTC Act. The general substantive provisions of consumer protection law generally are well established, and the FTC is acknowledged as an authority on these principles. States are free to go beyond, depart from, or even contradict the FTC's principles and interpretations in regulating unfair and deceptive practices, but absent an indication that this has been done, relevant FTC precedent is viewed by many state courts with some deference.[3]

A. General Provisions of State Consumer Protection Laws

1. Scope of the Statutes

Many state consumer protection statutes contain specific laws, provisions, or regulations dealing with particular practices or areas of commerce. At the same time, they contain general language that enables enforcers to respond to innovative or unanticipated tactics. Thus, the practitioner must be aware not only of what the applicable statutes indicate about a specific practice or product area under consideration, but also which general provision may govern the conduct at issue. Some state consumer protection statutes, however, explicitly exempt certain practices or industries that are already subject to regulation by other laws.[4] In other cases, extensive state regulation of a particular area of commerce may partly or wholly preempt the UDAP statute without explicit notice in the statute to this effect, or by a general provision in the UDAP statute exempting "regulated practices."[5]

---

[3]   *See infra* 3.A.3.

[4]   For example, New York's General Statute § 75-1.1 exempts professional services by a member of the "learned professions." N.Y. GEN. BUS. LAW § 75-1.1 (McKinney 2003). The Louisiana Unfair Trade Practices and Consumer Protection Law does not apply to "[a]ctions or transactions subject to the jurisdiction of the Louisiana Public Service Commission or other public utility regulatory body, the commissioner of financial institutions, the insurance commissioner, the financial institutions and insurance regulators of other states, or federal banking regulators who possess authority to regulate unfair or deceptive trade practices." LA. REV. STAT. § 51:1406 (West 2002).

[5]   For example, Massachusetts law provides that, "nothing in this chapter shall apply to transactions or actions otherwise permitted under laws as

Most state consumer protection laws or regulations provide a "laundry list" of practices that are deemed per se unfair or deceptive.[6] For example, in Illinois, the Consumer Fraud and Deceptive Practices Act enumerates several practices considered deceptive under its general definition.[7] Further, Illinois' implementation of its Uniform Deceptive Trade Practices Act adds eleven more specific deceptive trade practices.[8] Such per se unlawful prohibitions typically encompass well known deceptions, such as the classic "bait-and-switch" – or, as the statute puts it, "advertis[ing] goods or services with intent not to supply reasonably expectable public demand, unless the advertisement discloses a limitation of quantity."[9] A company's activities that are deemed to fall into one of the statute's enumerated categorical prohibitions will be found unlawful. As in any per se regime, however, there may be plenty to litigate before the act in question is found to fall into the category, such as whether the defendant had intent not to supply reasonably expectable public demand in the bait-and-switch example. Both the statute and its associated regulations should be checked for such a laundry list before commencing a litigation under an unfamiliar consumer protection statute, whether as plaintiff or defendant.

As a state's experience with particular practices grows, the body of case law and/or administrative regulations issued under state UDAP statutes may come to classify other types of activities as per se UDAP violations. Acts that violate other consumer-oriented laws are one class of such activities.[10] Established violations of the FTC Act or other statutes intended to protect consumers may be accepted by courts as violations of state consumer protection laws with little or no additional

---

      administered by any regulatory board or officer acting under statutory authority of the commonwealth or of the United States." MASS. GEN. LAWS ch. 93A, § 3 (2003).

[6]   As described below, many state UDAP statutes are due not provide for true per se liability, especially when enforced by private litigants as opposed to state Attorneys General, inasmuch as they may include one or more additional required elements such as intent to deceive, actual deception, materiality, reliance by the plaintiff, and injury. Laundry lists thus often create per se violations only in the limited sense that defenses may not be raised as to the conduct itself.

[7]   815 ILL. COMP. STAT. 505 (2003).

[8]   815 ILL. COMP. STAT. 510/2(a)(10) (2003).

[9]   *Id.*

[10]   *See, e.g.,* Yale New Haven Hosp. v. Mitchell, 683 A.2d 1362 (Conn. 1995) (holding that Connecticut UDAP law provides private right of action for violation of federal Hill-Burton Act, giving plaintiffs a private right of action where none existed under predicate statute).

proof or evidence required. For example, a regulation under the Massachusetts Consumer Protection Act renders any violation of any existing statute or regulation meant for the promotion of the public's health, safety, or welfare a violation of that law.[11] Other states have achieved a similar effect through judicial rulings, applying various different criteria to determine which federal or state laws can provide the predicate for a per se UDAP violation.[12] Connecticut courts, for example, have held that among the elements of a Connecticut Unfair Trade Practices violation is "whether the practice, without necessarily having been previously considered unlawful, offends public policy as it has been established by statutes, the common law, or otherwise--whether, in other words, it is within at least the penumbra of some common law, statutory, or other established concept of unfairness." [13] However, the Texas legislature has provided specifically that violations of other

---

[11]   MASS. REGS. CODE tit. 940, § 3.16 (2003).

[12]   Such states include Connecticut, Cheshire Mortgage Serv., Inc. v. Montes, 612 A.2d 1130, 1144 (Conn. 1992) (holding violations of the federal Truth in Lending Act and excessive prepaid finance charges in violation of Conn. Gen. Stat. § 36-224l to be violations of CUTPA); New York, In re Scrimpsher, 17 B.R. 999, 1017 (Bankr. N.D.N.Y. 1982) (party liable under § 349 of New York General Business Law for violations of Fair Debt Collection Practices Act); North Carolina, Winston Realty Co. v. G.H.G. Inc., 331 S.E.2d 677, 681 (N.C. 1985) (violation of N.C.G.S.A. § 75-1.1, prohibiting unfair or deceptive acts or practices, can be predicated on violation of N.C.G.S.A. § 95-47.6, prohibiting false advertising and false representations by personnel agencies); Pennsylvania, In re Fricker, 115 B.R. 809, 823 (Bankr. E.D. Pa. 1990) ("any conduct which constitutes a violation of criminal laws enacted for the protection of consumers, like the [Pennsylvania Debt Pooling Act], which creates significant confusion and misunderstanding ... must perforce be conduct prohibited by the catchall provision of UDAP"); In re Stewart, 93 B. R. 878, 887 (Bankr. E.D. Pa. 1988) (holding that violations of Pennsylvania Goods and Services Installment Sales Act and Truth in Lending Act are UDAP violations); and Washington, Salois v. Mutual of Omaha Ins. Co., 581 P.2d 1349, 1351-52 (1978) (consumer protection violation predicated on violation of state insurance code); State v. Reader's Digest Ass'n, Inc., 501 P.2d 290, 301-02 (1972) (conduct is per se unfair trade practice if (1) the action is illegal and (2) it is against public policy as declared by the legislature or the judiciary).

[13]   Web Press Serv. Corp. v. New London Motors, Inc., 525 A.2d 57, *later appeal*, 533 A.2d 1211 (Conn. 1987), quoting McLaughlin Ford, Inc. v. Ford Motor Co., 473 A.2d 1185 (Conn. 1984), quoting Conaway v. Prestia, 464 A.2d 847 (Conn. 1983), quoting FTC v. Sperry & Hutchinson Co., 405 U.S. 233, 244-45 n. (1972).

consumer-oriented statutes do *not* necessarily constitute UDAP violations.[14]

In addition, a state's other consumer-oriented statutes may themselves refer to its UDAP statute, providing that any violation of those statutes also constitutes a UDAP violation. In Connecticut, for example, violations of the Connecticut Retail Purchase Statute,[15] the Trade Names statute,[16] the law governing community association managers,[17] and the statute regulating health clubs,[18] among others, are deemed unfair and deceptive trade practices in violation of Connecticut's UDAP statute.

2. *Intent, Deception, Reliance, and Injury*

Most state consumer protection statutes, like the FTC Act, do not require proof that the wrongdoer had any fraudulent knowledge or intent. However, a few states have imposed such a requirement. For instance, Arkansas and Wyoming laws prohibit false representations as to the characteristics of goods or services only if *knowingly* made.[19] Colorado, Indiana, Kansas, Nevada, and Oklahoma, using various formulations, prohibit false advertising claims only if the claimer *knows or should know* that the claims are false.[20] Similarly, while Oregon's UDAP law makes false representations about goods and services unlawful without reference to the defendant's state of mind,[21] it affords a private right of action only to "any person who suffers any ascertainable loss…as a result of *willful* use or employment by another person of a method, act or practice declared unlawful,"[22] South Dakota declares it a "deceptive act or practice" only when a person "knowingly and intentionally" acts, uses or employs a deceptive act or practice.[23] Utah law finds a violation only if a person commits a deceptive act or practice "with intent to deceive."[24]

---

[14]   *See* TEX. BUS. & COM. CODE ANN. § 17.43 (Vernon 2003).

[15]   CONN. GEN. STAT. § 42-251 (2003).

[16]   CONN. GEN. STAT. § 35-1 (2003).

[17]   CONN. GEN. STAT. § 20-257(b) (2003).

[18]   CONN. GEN. STAT. § 21a-222(b) (2003).

[19]   ARK. CODE ANN. § 4-88-107(a)(1) (2003); WYO. STAT. ANN. § 40-12-105(a) (Michie 2002).

[20]   COLO. REV. STAT. § 6-1-105(1) (2003); IND. CODE § 24-5-0.5.3(a) (2003); KAN. STAT. ANN. § 50-626(b) (2002); NEV. REV. STAT. 598.410 (2003); OKLA. STAT. tit. 15, § 753 (2002).

[21]   ORE. REV. STAT. § 646.608(1) (2001).

[22]   ORE. REV. STAT. § 646.638(1) (2001) (emphasis added).

[23]   S.D. CODIFIED LAWS ANN. § 37-24-6 (Michie 2003)

[24]   UTAH CODE ANN. § 13-11-4 (2003).

Most states require that an individual plaintiff seeking damages prove that he or she relied on the false representations associated with the deceptive practice; judicial rulings to this effect have occurred in Arizona,[25] Georgia,[26] Indiana,[27] and Wyoming.[28] Other state courts require that the plaintiff prove that the deceptive practice proximately caused the plaintiff's injury, a showing that generally implies reliance.[29] Some states have carved out a limited exception for class actions, holding that individual proof of reliance is not necessary under certain circumstances, such as when the alleged deceptive misrepresentations took the form of "standardized forms or routinized procedures."[30] Such rulings tend to facilitate the resolution of these types of consumer protection violations through class actions.

3. Value of FTC Precedent

Many states have enacted legislation that closely follows Section 5 of the FTC Act. As described below, several of these states expressly provide that their consumer protection acts will be construed consistently with the interpretations of the FTC Act issued by the Federal Trade Commission and the federal courts. These statutes are commonly termed "little FTC Acts."

State and local jurisdictions ascribe varying degrees of deference to decisions under the FTC Act and to FTC rules and policy statements.

---

[25] *See* Peery v. Hansen, 585 P.2d 574, 577 (Ariz. Ct. App. 1978); Holeman v. Neils, 803 F. Supp. 237, 242-43 (D. Ariz. 1992).

[26] *See* Delta Chevrolet v. Willis, 371 S.E.2d 250 (Ga. App. 1988) (conclusively presuming plaintiffs read written car leases and therefore did not rely on oral misrepresentations); Zeeman v. Black, 273 S.E.2d 910, 916 (Ga. App. 1980).

[27] IND. CODE § 24-5-0.5-4 (2003) (limiting damages to those "relying upon" a deceptive act).

[28] WYO. STAT. ANN. §40-12-108(a) (Michie 2002) (limiting damages to those "relying upon" a deceptive act).

[29] *See, e.g.*, Oliveira v. Amoco Oil Co. 776 N.E.2d 151, 155 (Ill. 2002) (holding that "section 10a(a) [of the ICFA] imposes an obligation upon a private individual seeking actual damages under the Act to 'demonstrate that the fraud complained of proximately caused' those damages in order to recover for his injury"); Zekman v. Direct Am. Marketers, Inc., 695 N.E.2d 853, 860-62 (Ill. 1998) (requiring that "a successful claim by a private individual suing under the Act must ... demonstrate that the fraud complained of proximately caused plaintiff's injury").

[30] *See, e.g.*, Washington v. Spitzer Mgmt., Inc., 2003 Ohio 1735, ¶¶ 34-37, 2003 WL 1759617, at *6 (Ohio Ct. App. Apr. 3, 2003); *see also* Alford Chevrolet-Geo v. Jones, 91 S.W.3d 396, 404 (Tex. App. 2002).

Most state consumer protection statutes are modeled after the FTC Act to a greater or lesser degree, ranging from near-exact copies ("little FTC Acts," discussed below), to statutes merely influenced in part by the FTC Act. Most stage legislatures intended that these statutes should build on the work accomplished by the FTC. Accordingly, state consumer protection statutes commonly include a provision along the lines of, "It is the intent of the legislature that in construing this Act, the courts will be guided by the interpretations given by the Federal Trade Commission and the federal courts to Section 5(a)(1) of the Federal Trade Commission Act (15 U.S.C. 45(a)(1))." States enacting a similar provision, or that have had a judicial ruling to the same effect, include Alabama,[31] Alaska,[32] Arizona,[33] Connecticut,[34] Florida,[35] Georgia,[36] Hawaii,[37] Idaho,[38] Illinois,[39] Louisiana,[40] Maine,[41] Maryland,[42] Massachusetts,[43] Montana,[44] New Hampshire,[45] New Mexico,[46] New York,[47] Ohio,[48] Rhode Island,[49] South Carolina,[50] Tennessee,[51] Texas,[52]

---

[31]   ALA. CODE. § 8-19-6 (2003).

[32]   ALASKA STAT. § 45.50.545 (Michie 2002).

[33]   ARIZ. REV. STAT. § 44-1522 (2003).

[34]   CONN. GEN. STAT. § 42-110b(b)-(c) (2003).

[35]   FLA. STAT. ch. 501.204 (2003).

[36]   GA. CODE § 10-1-391 (2003).

[37]   HAW. REV. STAT. § 480-2(b) (2003).

[38]   IDAHO CODE § 48-604 (Michie 2003).

[39]   815 ILL. COMP. STAT. 505/2 (2003).

[40]   LA. REV. STAT. § 51:1406 (2002).

[41]   ME. REV. STAT. tit 5, § 207 (West 2003).

[42]   MD. CODE ANN., COM. LAW I § 13-105 (2003).

[43]   MASS GEN. LAWS ch. 93A, § 2(b)-(c) (2003).

[44]   MONT. CODE § 30-14-104 (2003).

[45]   N.H. REV. STAT. ANN. § 358-A:13 (2003).

[46]   N.M. STAT. ANN. § 57-12-4 (2003).

[47]   State v. Colo. State Christian College, 76 Misc. 2d 50, 54-55 (N.Y. Sup. Ct. 1973) ("the intention of the New York Legislature in enacting § 349 of the General Business Law was to follow in the steps of the Federal Trade Commission with respect to the interpretation of deceptive acts and practices outlawed in Section 5 of the Federal Trade Commission Act"). In an action brought by the New York Attorney General alleging violations of § 349 or § 350, it is a complete defense that the act, practice, or advertisement is "subject to and complies with the rules and regulations of, and the statutes administered by, the [F]ederal [T]rade [C]ommission." N.Y. GEN. BUS. LAW §§ 349(d), 350(d) (McKinney 2003).

[48]   OHIO REV. CODE § 1345.02(c) (West 2003).

[49]   R.I. GEN. LAW s§ 6-13.1-3 (2002).

[50]   S.C. CODE ANN. § 39-5-20(b) (Law Co-op. 2003).

Vermont,[53] Washington,[54] and West Virginia.[55] Even in jurisdictions where no deference is given to FTC Act precedent as a formal matter, citing cases under the FTC Act may well be persuasive.

When the state consumer protection statute is not a little FTC Act, but nevertheless relies on the FTC Act for interpretation, it can sometimes be difficult to apply the FTC Act rulings and pronouncements. For example, some state consumer protection statutes condemn deceptive practices but not "unfair" ones, and it has not always been clear whether particular practices before the FTC would be classified as unfair or as deceptive.[56]

FTC rules, guides, and other materials not having the formal precedential impact of administrative or federal court rulings also are used in interpreting state consumer protection laws, as indicated in the typical provision quoted above.

4. Other State Consumer Protection Precedent

Many state consumer protection statutes are modeled after the FTC Act, model acts, or the acts of other states. Where another state's statute contains substantially the same language, courts may be persuaded by precedent interpreting that similar language in other states. This is at the discretion of the state court, and is likely to depend on factors such as an absence of case law or legislative history concerning the relevant language in the home state, the detail with which the language has been interpreted in the other state, and the general degree of respect held by the court in question for the other state's approach to consumer protection enforcement.[57]

5. Uniform Deceptive Trade Practices Act

The Uniform Deceptive Trade Practices Act (UDTPA) was drafted in 1964 and revised in 1966 by the National Conference of

---

[51]   TENN. CODE ANN. § 47-18-115 (2003).

[52]   TEX. BUS. & COM. CODE § 17.46(c)(1) (2003).

[53]   VT. STAT. ANN. tit. 9, § 2453 (2003).

[54]   WASH. REV. CODE § 19.86.920 (2003).

[55]   W. VA. CODE § 46A-6-103 (2003).

[56]   *See supra* 1.C.

[57]   *See* Normand Josef Enters., Inc. v. Conn. Nat'l. Bank, 646 A.2d 1289, 1306 (Conn. 1994) (noting that the Connecticut Supreme Court has "repeatedly looked to the reasoning and decisions of the Supreme Judicial Court of Massachusetts with regard to the scope of [Connecticut Unfair Trade Practices Act]").

Commissioners on Uniform State Laws. Broadly, the UDTPA addresses the following practices:

- Passing off goods or services as those of another or causing likelihood of confusion or misunderstanding as to the source or approval of goods or services;
- Deceptive representations or designations of goods as to their geographic source, sponsorship, approval, characteristics, ingredients, uses or benefits, quality or grade, status as original or new;
- Disparagement of the goods, services or business of someone else by false or misleading representations;
- "Bait-and-switch" advertising; and
- False or misleading statements concerning the reasons for or the existence of price reduction.

In addition, the UDTPA prohibits any other conduct that similarly creates a likelihood of confusion or of misunderstanding.

Like the Lanham Act, the UDTPA has a dual focus. Some of its provisions appear designed primarily to protect competitors, focusing on traditional trademark and trade dress infringement issues such as passing off another's product as one's own or disparaging another's product. Other provisions address deceptive trade practices that are intended mainly to deceive consumers. These latter practices injure competitors only insofar as the competitive advantage gained by being able to exaggerate or misrepresent one's products or prices creates an uneven playing field compared with honest competitors. In both areas, the UDTPA was intended to codify common law causes of action.

Several states have adopted the UDTPA in either its 1964 or 1966 form, including Colorado, Delaware, Georgia, Hawaii, Illinois, Maine, Minnesota, Nebraska, New Mexico, Ohio, Oklahoma, and Oregon.[58] Other states' laws have also been influenced by its provisions.[59] However, as with most "uniform" statutes, states have modified the

---

[58]   COLO. REV. STAT. §§ 6-1-101 to 6-1-115 (2003); DEL. CODE. ANN., tit. 6 §§ 2531 to 2536 (2003); GA. CODE. ANN. §§ 10-1-370 to 10-1-375 (2003); HAW. REV. STAT. §§ 481A-1 to 481A-5 (2003); 815 ILL. COMP. STAT. 510; ME. REV. STAT. ANN. tit. 10, §§ 1211 to 1216 (2003); MINN. STAT. ANN. §§ 325D.43 to 325D.48 (2003); NEB. REV. STAT. §§ 87-301 to 87-306 (2003); N.M. STAT. ANN. §§ 57-12-1 *et seq.* (2003); OHIO REV. CODE ANN. § 4165 (West 2003); OKLA. STAT. ANN. tit. 78 §§ 51 to 55 (West 2003); OR. REV. STAT. §§ 646.605 to 646.656 (2001).

[59]   For example, Pennsylvania has incorporated the enumerated practices of the UDTPA into its Unfair Trade Practices and Consumer Protection law, PA. STAT. ANN. tit. 73, § 201-2 (West 2003).

UDTPA in a number of ways, including enumerating additional violations. In addition, some states have enacted additional consumer protection statutes that coexist with their versions of the UDTPA, often covering many of the same practices.[60]

Though the UDTPA was primarily intended to provide a right of action for business competitors, statutes that follow the UDTPA may provide that "a plaintiff need not prove competition between the parties," but only that the plaintiff must be "likely to be damaged."[61] Courts in some states that have enacted the UDTPA have allowed private, consumer causes of action to be maintained.[62] Plaintiffs in such actions may obtain injunctive relief, litigation costs, and – if the deception was knowing – attorney's fees.[63] There is no right of recovery for damages under the UDPTA, a fact that has largely limited the application of this statute to situations where injunctive relief is important to the plaintiff and the state lacks any other law providing for a private plaintiff to pursue the violation in question. Where a complained-of practice falls into one of the enumerated offenses under the UDTPA, plaintiffs frequently will plead violations under both UDTPA and the state's other UDAP statute, seeking to use a UDTPA violation to establish a per se case for damages under the UDAP law.

6. California Business and Professions Code Section 17200

California's consumer protection statute, known as Section 17200,[64] warrants special mention because of the breadth of the statute, California's importance as a commercial state, and the enforcement

---

[60] *See, e.g.*, Illinois Consumer Fraud and Deceptive Business Practices Act, 815 ILL. COMP. STAT. 505 (2003).

[61] 815 ILL. COMP. STAT. 510/2 (2003).

[62] *See, e.g.,* Garland v. Mobil Oil Corp., 340 F. Supp. 1095 (N.D. Ill. 1972); Searcy v. Bend Garage Co., 592 P.2d 558 (Or. 1979); Roberts v. Am. Warranty Corp., 514 A.2d 1132, 1134 (Del. Super. Ct. 1986); Williams v. Bruno Appliance & Furniture Mart, 379 N.E.2d 52 (Ill. App. 1978). *But see* Wald v. Wilmington Trust Co., 552 A.2d 853, 855 (Del. Super. Ct. 1988) (holding consumer treble damage remedy not available under Delaware UDTPA); Trabardo v. Kenton Ruritan Club Inc., 517 A.2d 706, 709 (Del. Super. Ct. 1986) ("Under the Act, a remedy for damages may be available to one who has a business or trade interest at stake, but not to a mere consumer."); Glazewski v. Coronet Ins. Co., 483 N.E.2d 1263, 1267 (Ill. 1985) (finding that allegations of violation of Uniform Act do not support action for damages).

[63] *See infra* 3.C.1.b.

[64] CAL. BUS. & PROF. CODE §§ 17200 *et seq.* (West 2003).

activism of both the Attorney General's office and private plaintiffs within the state.

Section 17200 prohibits "[u]ntrue or misleading statements and unfair methods of competition including unfair, fraudulent or unlawful business practices and deceptive advertising."[65] This combines most of the types of violations defined by various state UDAP laws into a single statement, with a significant addition. Because Section 17200 prohibits "unlawful" business practices, it has been interpreted to establish a private right of action for any business practice that violates any other California law.[66]

The other unique feature of 17200 is who may sue. The relevant provision confers standing on "any person acting for the interests of itself, its members or the general public."[67] Any person, whether or not injured by the practice, may sue under the statute for injunctive relief, other affirmative equitable relief such as appointment of receivers or remedial practices, restitution, and in egregious cases, punitive damages. In California parlance, this provision potential makes any person a "private attorney general" who can enforce virtually any law regulating business.

Section 17200 has been so broadly interpreted and widely used that California Attorney General William Lockyer has begun filing § 17200 claims against law firms for their own alleged abuses of § 17200. On February 26, 2003, the state of California sued a Beverly Hills firm accused of extorting money from thousands of small businesses by filing frivolous § 17200 suits and then promptly offering the businesses an opportunity to buy their way out of litigation for several thousand dollars.[68]

B. STATE ATTORNEY GENERAL ENFORCEMENT

Almost all state consumer protection statutes empower the state's Attorney General to enforce their provisions, in addition to any private remedies that they may provide. Presently, the exceptions are Georgia and Hawaii, but these states' consumer protection laws empower other

---

[65]   *Id.*

[66]   Stop Youth Addiction v. Lucky Stores, Inc., 950 P.2d 1086, 1090-91 (Cal. 1998) (confirming that a cause of action could be asserted by any citizen under § 17200 for violation of another statute which did not itself have a private right of action).

[67]   CAL. BUS. & PROF. CODE § 17204 (West 2003).

[68]   People v. Trevor Law Group LLP (Cal. App. Dep't. Super. Ct. filed Feb. 26, 2003); *see also* the California Attorney General's website, http://ag.ca.gov/newsalerts/2003/03-021.htm.

government bodies to enforce the statutes in the place of the Attorney General.[69] Of the others, every state conducts its consumer protection enforcement somewhat differently. For the practitioner, even more important than the formal differences in consumer protection powers and responsibilities assigned by each state to its Attorney General are the varying levels of activism from state to state.

1. Enforcement Powers and Procedures

Like the FTC, Attorneys General often commence consumer protection actions with an investigation phase, during which they have access to compulsory process.[70] The most common tools are the civil investigative demand (CID) and the traditional subpoena. Generally, Attorneys General are given broad authority to employ these tools without interference by the state's courts. Virtually any relevant information may be sought and obtained, even if not entirely material to the investigation, except to the extent that the burden of responding will seriously hinder the respondent's normal business operations.[71] States vary on the extent to which they will demand production of information even though it is confidential or a trade secret.[72] The courts of the state typically find that concerns about confidentiality of the information being disclosed can be handled through designation of the material as confidential and through representations by the Attorney General that the information will not be disclosed.

UDAP statutes themselves may provide special rules and procedures for discovery in cases brought under those laws. These procedures may

---

[69] In Georgia, the Administrator of the Fair Business Act, appointed pursuant to O.C.G.A. 10-1-395, is statutorily authorized to undertake consumer protection functions. In Hawaii, the Office of Consumer Protection, though not part of the Attorney General's Office, is authorized to represent the State of Hawaii in consumer protection actions. In addition, the District of Columbia, which has no Attorney General, may be represented in consumer protection actions by its Corporation Counsel under D.C. Code § 28-3909. The comments in this section that reference Attorneys General also apply, in most cases, to these entities.

[70] *See, e.g.,* NEB. REV. STAT. § 87-303 (2003) (establishing Nebraska Attorney General's subpoena powers under Nebraska's Uniform Deceptive Trade Practices Act).

[71] The FTC precedent in this regard is typical of those under state case law, where this issue has been examined. *See, e.g.,* FTC v. Jim Walter Corp., 651 F.2d 251 (5th Cir. 1981).

[72] *See, e.g., In re* Yankee Milk, 372 Mass. 353 (1977) (outlining Massachusetts six-factor test for discoverability of trade secrets by investigating Attorney General).

allow forms of discovery not normally available to a plaintiff or investigator, such as precomplaint depositions. Respondents, on the other hand, have no right in most states to conduct discovery into the progress of the Attorney General's investigation. Much of this information is generally held protected under some form of investigatory privilege.[73]

Like the FTC, state Attorneys General may also conduct what amount to sting operations by having staff members pose as consumers to provide direct evidence of the transgression being investigated.[74]

Under the authority of a 1980 amendment to the FTC Act, the FTC can work with state Attorneys General in cooperative investigations. The revised Act provides for the sharing with the states (and local law enforcement) the FTC's investigatory records and evidence.[75] Essentially, this information can be used freely by such agencies for investigation, and also for most litigation purposes. Such cooperation is now routine, as discussed above, especially during broad sweeps of specific types of rampant consumer protection violation.[76]

These basic parameters of state Attorney General UDAP enforcement may give the appearance of being weighted against the respondent, and this is not far from the truth. State legislatures take their obligations to consumers seriously, and have endowed Attorneys General with extensive powers. Typically, only a few mechanisms to protect the respondent are in place. Some states, for example, require that the target of the investigation be notified and given the opportunity to comply voluntarily with the state's wishes before an enforcement action can be commenced.[77]

---

[73]   *See, e.g.,* People v. Volkswagen of Am. Inc., 342 N.Y.S.2d 749, 749 (N.Y. App. Div. 1973) (holding defendant not entitled to New York Attorney General's UDAP investigatory information under investigatory privilege).

[74]   For example, Project Busted Opportunity is a joint FTC-state sting operation in which investigators from both the FTC and state Attorneys General's offices posed as victims of business opportunity scams, resulting in the filing of numerous state lawsuits. *See* Fed. Trade Comm'n, *State, Federal Law Enforcers Launch Sting on Business Opportunity, Work-at-Home Scams, available at* http://www.ftc.gov/opa/2002/06/bizopswe.htm.

[75]   15 U.S.C. § 46(f).

[76]   *See supra* 2.A.2.a.2.

[77]   *See, e.g.,* N.Y. GEN. BUS. LAW § 349(c) (2003) (with respect to deceptive acts or practices, "[b]efore any violation of this section is sought to be enjoined, the attorney general shall be required to give the person against whom such proceeding is contemplated notice by certified mail and an opportunity to show in writing within five business days after receipt of

Generally, a state Attorney General empowered to enforce UDAP laws may act on any violation of the statute as outlined above. Attorney General enforcement powers often are even broader than available consumer remedies. In states where consumers must suffer actual deception or injury to have a cause of action, these requirements typically do not apply to the Attorney General.[78] Attorneys General also can sometimes sue on behalf of constituencies other than consumers, such as business customers, whether or not these business customers would have a right of action under the statute.[79]

2. Remedies

a. Injunctive Relief

The most important priority for state Attorneys General is stopping the unfair or deceptive practice at issue. To this end, all states empower their Attorneys General to seek cease-and-desist orders enjoining such practices. Attorney Generals may seek "fencing-in" injunctive provisions that are broader than the challenged conduct and encompassing conduct that might otherwise be lawful, in the same manner and for the same reasons as the FTC. In extreme cases, an

---

notice why proceedings should not be instituted against him, unless the attorney general shall find, in any case in which he seeks preliminary relief, that to give such notice and opportunity is not in the public interest"); N.Y. GEN. BUS. LAW § 350(c) (2003) (with respect to false advertising, "[b]efore the attorney general commences an action [for civil penalties] he shall be required to give the person against whom such action is contemplated appropriate notice by certified mail and an opportunity to show, either orally or in writing, why such action should not be commenced").

[78]   *See, e.g.,* Duran v. Leslie Oldsmobile, Inc., 594 N.E.2d 1355, 1362 (Ill. App. Ct. 1992) ("just as with damages, reliance remains an element of a private cause of action [under Illinois' Consumer Fraud Act] although it has been eliminated as a requirement for actions brought by the Attorney General").

[79]   *See, e.g.,* Ferguson v. Beal, 588 S.W.2d 651 (Tex. App. 1979) (holding Texas Attorney General may sue where real estate purchasers would not have a claim); Commonwealth *ex rel.* Stephens v. North American Van Lines, Inc., 600 S.W.2d 459 (Ky. Ct. App. 1979) (holding Kentucky Attorney General may sue where purchasers were not consumers and would not have a claim); People *ex rel.* Fahner v. Walsh, 461 N.E.2d 78, 82 (Ill. App. 1984) (holding same for Illinois).

offender can be banished from doing business in the state,[80] or placed under such restrictions that for practical purposes it is impossible to continue in business.[81]

Where advertising is concerned, the limited Constitutional rights of free commercial speech come into play.[82] However, as discussed above, once a commercial claim (as opposed to political or other "core" speech) has been found deceptive, it ceases to have any Constitutional protection and may be enjoined.[83] It is also generally considered Constitutional to issue an injunction requiring that a violator's future advertising claims be substantiated.[84] Affirmative actions may also be required by an injunctive order in a state UDAP case, such as corrective advertising or packaging or the disclosure to potential customers that the violator has committed unfair or deceptive practices in the past.[85]

Attorneys General may pursue preliminary injunctions to halt a challenged practice as quickly as possible, usually under the standards prevailing in the relevant jurisdiction for such relief. Many Attorneys General have access to the same other equitable remedies, such as freezing of assets or appointment of receivers, that are available to the FTC.[86]

It is not a defense to an action for injunctive relief that the defendant has already ceased the challenged practice. Like the FTC, states are granted broad latitude in prohibiting acts that a wily defendant is free to resume in the future.

When a preliminary or permanent injunction is violated, Attorneys General may sue, civilly and/or criminally depending on the jurisdiction, to enforce the order and for additional penalties for contempt. Some

---

[80] *See, e.g.,* State v. Koscot Interplanetary Inc., 212 Kan. 688 (1973) (ordering company not to do business in the Kansas).

[81] *See, e.g.,* Kugler v. Haitian Tours, Inc., 120 N.J. Super. 260 (N.J. Super. Ch. 1972) (enjoining company from selling its only product).

[82] *See supra* 1.B.13.

[83] *See* Zauderer v. Office of Disciplinary Counsel, 471 U.S. 626 (1985).

[84] *See* People v. Custom Craft Carpets, Inc., 206 Cal. Rptr. 12 (Ct. App. 1984).

[85] *See, e.g.,* Consumers Union v. Alta-Dena Certified Dairy, 4 Cal. App. 4th 963 (1992) (forcing advertiser in § 17200 case to make affirmative statements to undo effects of prior false statements); Complaint, Ohio *ex rel.* Betty D. Montgomery v. Philip Morris, No. 97CVH05 5114 (Ct. of Common Pleas, Franklin Cty., Ohio May 8, 1997) (seeking, *inter alia*, corrective advertising for alleged Ohio Consumer Sales Practices Act violation), *available at* http://stic.neu.edu/Oh/tobacco.htm.

[86] *See, e.g.,* CONN. GEN. STAT. §§ 42-110f, 42-110m (2003) (providing for powers of receiver appointed under Connecticut Unfair Trade Practices Act).

UDAP statutes impose specific monetary penalties for violations of an injunction, while others leave the penalty up to the litigants and the court.[87] Most statutory penalties are assessed on a per-violation basis, so they can be multiplied many times as the result of a single enforcement proceeding. Prison terms for offenders are also occasionally awarded.[88]

b. Monetary Relief

Most states also permit Attorneys General to seek to recover monetary restitution in addition to injunctive relief.[89] Statutes vary widely in the amount of monetary relief they authorize and in their imposition of additional conditions, such as willful or knowing violation. Some statutes do not provide for specific dollar penalties, and those that do often provide for per-violation assessment that can lead to multiple awards, so the total financial penalty for a given respondent is almost always uncertain *ex ante*. In some cases, courts have assessed the monetary penalty once (or even more than once) for each customer or consumer estimated to have been harmed by the practice.[90] This gives a court flexibility to impose almost any desired penalty.

Restitution awards are generally repaid to consumers in some form. If the violator has customer records, it can be required to repay the funds directly. In other situations, various forms of notice are employed and consumers are permitted to claim their restitution from a fund paid by the defendant. Where the monetary awards are too diffuse to justify the transaction costs in returning it to consumers or the consumers cannot be identified, in some states the funds may be retained by the state and used for public purposes, often related in some way to the challenged practice.[91] The state may also be able to recoup its attorney fees.[92]

---

[87]   *See, e.g.,* CONN. GEN. STAT. § 42-110o (2003) (providing that the Connecticut Attorney General may seek civil penalties of up to $25,000 per violation of the Connecticut Unfair Trade Practices Act).

[88]   *See, e.g.,* Commonwealth v. Vergotz, 616 A.2d 1379, 1382 (Pa. Super. Ct. 1992) (upholding one- to two-year prison term for illegal sale of auto inspection stickers in violation of Pennsylvania Deceptive Business Practices Act).

[89]   *See, e.g.,* CONN. GEN. STAT. §§ 42-110d, 42-110m (2003) (providing that Connecticut Attorney General or Commissioner of Consumer Protection may seek restitution, in addition to any other remedies, for alleged violations of the Connecticut Unfair Trade Practices Act).

[90]   *See, e.g.,* People v. Bestline Prods. Inc., 61 Cal. App. 3d 879 (1976); People v. Toomey, 157 Cal. App. 3d 1 (1984).

[91]   *See, e.g.,* MINN. STAT. ANN. § 8.31.2C (2003).

[92]   *See, e.g.,* Commonwealth v. Fall River Motor Sales, Inc., 409 Mass. 302 (1991).

3. Other State Laws

State Attorneys General are also charged with enforcing state laws in all other areas of commerce. These can include many laws that have a consumer orientation or that touch upon issues discussed in this handbook, including online privacy, credit and other consumer transactions, and advertising. In addition, states routinely pass laws regulating specific industries or commercial sectors.[93] Each of these laws is unique, and it is impractical even to sketch them here.

For the practitioner lacking access to specialized resources on state consumer protection law, the best way to begin the determination of which statutes exist and are being actively enforced in a given state often is to locate the Attorney General's Internet website. Attorneys General's sites invariably feature consumer protection prominently and usually provide press releases, summaries of decisions, and often the decisions and underlying statutes themselves.[94] The sites often include guides for businesses, and invariably contain contact information so that the Attorney General's office can be contacted directly.

4. Local Laws

Localities also sometimes regulate consumer protection. Typical areas of local regulation include item price and discount advertising, return policies, and other advertising that is likely to be created at the local or retail level. Many localities are also empowered to challenge false and misleading advertising, often as part of their authority to license local businesses.[95] New York City's Department of Consumer Affairs, for example, enforces the city's Consumer Protection Law, which forbids all "deceptive or unconscionable trade practices in the sale, lease, rental

---

[93] New York, for example, regulates industries such as agriculture (N.Y. AGRIC. & MKTS. LAW §§ 1 to 500 (McKinney 2003)), alcoholic beverages (N.Y. ALCO. BEV. CONT. LAW §§ 1 to 164 (McKinney 2003)), banking (N.Y. BANKING LAW §§ 1 to 9019 (McKinney 2003)), energy (N.Y. ENERGY LAW §§ 1-101 to 21-106 (McKinney 2003)), insurance (N.Y. INS. LAW §§ 101 to 9901 (McKinney 2003)), and railroads (N.Y. R.R. LAW §§ 1 to 451 (McKinney 2003)), among others.

[94] *See, e.g.,* the New York Attorney General's website at http://www.oag.state.ny.us; the California Attorney General's website at http://caag.state.ca.us; the Texas Attorney General's website at http://www.oag.state.tx.us.

[95] New York licenses at least 55 specific commercial categories ranging from general vendors to horse-drawn taxis. *See* http://www.nyc.gov/html/dca/html/dcalicat.html.

or loan or in the offering for sale, lease, rental, or loan of any consumer goods and services, or in the collection of consumer debts."[96] Localities also often have consumer-oriented laws and regulations governing specific industries.[97]

In the privacy area, San Francisco became at least the seventh jurisdiction within California to pass privacy legislation, requiring financial institutions that do business or have customers in San Francisco to provide notice and obtain explicit consent before disclosing customers' confidential information.[98] Some of these laws have been challenged by banks arguing that they are preempted by federal legislation such as the Fair Credit Reporting Act.[99] For the present, however, they continue to be enforced.

C. Private Actions under State Consumer Protection Laws

5. *Little FTC Acts and UDAP Statutes*

a. Private Right of Action for Consumers

Most state little FTC Acts and UDAP statutes explicitly provide for a private right of action and include varying degrees of guidance on who has standing, any special requirements for recovery, and the types of potential recovery within the text of the statutes or rules. A few states do not provide for a right of recovery by consumers, but have instituted one through judicial rulings. These states include Arizona,[100] Delaware,[101] and possibly Arkansas.[102]

---

[96] OFFICIAL COMPILATION OF THE RULES OF THE CITY OF NEW YORK, Title 6, Chapter 5. In December 2002, New York City announced a $4 million settlement with the H&R Block tax preparation company relating to alleged misrepresentations concerning H&R Block's Refund Anticipation Loan program. *See* http://www.nyc.gov/html/dca/pdf/hr_block.pdf.

[97] For example, in the New York City H&R Block settlement, violations of the city's Income Tax Preparer's Law, NEW YORK CITY ADMIN. CODE, Subch.8 §§ 20-739 to 29-743.1.

[98] Financial Information Privacy Ordinance, SAN FRANCISCO MUNICIPAL CODES Art. 20 §§ 2000-2010.

[99] *See, e.g.,* Complaint, Bank of Am. v. Daly City, No. 02-04343 CW (N.D. Cal. filed Sept. 11, 2002).

[100] *See* Sellinger v. Freeway Mobil Home Sales, 521 P.2d 1119, 1122 (Ariz. 1974).

[101] *See* Young v. Joyce, 351 A.2d 857 (Del. 1975).

[102] *See* Berkeley Pump Co. v. Reed-Joseph Land Co., 653 S.W.2d 128 (Ark. 1983).

Only a few states explicitly do not allow class actions under their UDAP statutes.[103] Class actions are generally possible, depending on the nature of the claim and damages asserted, and are subject to the state's rules and procedures for maintaining such actions.

b. Damages

Almost all states provide a right of recovery by consumers of actual monetary damages for UDAP violations. The purpose behind most deceptive practices is to induce consumers to purchase a product or service; accordingly, monetary damages are most often computed as the amount spent by consumers on these products or services.

Most states provide for enhanced damages in egregious cases. The most common formula is to increase damages, at the court's discretion, up to treble the actual monetary damages in egregious cases. This is the rule in Alabama, Alaska, Colorado, the District of Columbia, Hawaii, Louisiana, Massachusetts, Montana, New Hampshire, New Jersey, New Mexico, New York, North Carolina, North Dakota, Ohio, Pennsylvania, South Carolina, Tennessee, Vermont, and Washington.[104] Texas provides for double damages up to a cap of $1,000.[105] Other states provide for punitive damages with no limitation on the amount, giving courts flexibility in awarding these damages. Examples are California,

---

[103] E.g., Montana, *see* MONT. CODE ANN. § 30-14-133(1) (2003).

[104] *See* ALA. CODE § 8-19-10(a)(3) (2003); ALASKA STAT. § 45.50.531(a) (2002); COLO. REV. STAT. § 6-1-113(3) (2003); Robinson v. Lynmar Racquet Club, Inc., 851 P.2d 274 (Colo. Ct. App. 1993) (finding only single damages available in class actions, while up to treble damages are available in individual actions); D.C. CODE ANN. § 28-3905(k)(1) (2003); HAW. REV. STAT. § 480-13(b)(1) (2003); LA. REV. STAT. ANN. § 1409(A) (2002); MASS. GEN. LAWS ch. 93A, § 9(3) (2003); MONT. CODE ANN. § 30-14-133(1) (2003) (individual actions only); N.H. REV. STAT. ANN. § 358-A:10(l) (2003); N.J. REV. STAT. § 56:8-19 (2003); N.M. STAT. ANN. 57-12-10.E (2003) (but in class actions, only named plaintiffs may recover treble damages); N.Y. GEN. BUS. LAW § 349(h) (2003) (but with cap of $1,000 on treble damages); N.C. GEN. STAT. § 75-16 (2003); N.D. CENT. CODE § 51-15-09 (2003); OHIO REV. CODE ANN. § 1345.09(B) (2003) (but not available in class actions); PENN. STAT. § 201-9.2 (2003); S.C. CODE ANN. § 39-5-140(a) (2003); TENN. CODE ANN. § 47-18-109(a)(3) (2003); VT. STAT. ANN. tit. 9, § 2461 (2003); WASH. REV. CODE § 19.86.090 (2003).

[105] *See* TEX. BUS. & COM. CODE ANN. § 17.50(b)(1) (2003).

Connecticut, Georgia, Idaho, Kentucky, Missouri, Oregon, and Rhode Island.[106]

Still other states do not provide for extra or punitive damages except, in some states, the plaintiffs' costs and fees. These jurisdictions include Florida, Illinois, Indiana, Kansas, Maine, Maryland, Michigan, Minnesota, Mississippi, Nebraska, Nevada, Oklahoma, South Dakota, Utah, Virginia, West Virginia, Wisconsin, and Wyoming.[107] This, however, does not mean that a recovery in these states can never be more than actual damages plus costs and fees. The courts of many of these states have embraced the concept of fluid recovery and also have various forms of relief in equity at their disposal. They may, therefore, be able to increase awards well beyond actual damages on suitable occasions.

6. Common Law Fraud

Common-law fraud, deceit, or misrepresentation claims are commonly appended to complaints under UDAP statutes. As discussed above, these claims have one major drawback: the necessity to prove the intent to deceive, actual reliance, and injury. Weighing against this drawback are two major advantages: (1) a greater likelihood of recovering punitive damages if successful, and (2) broad applicability that may reach types of transactions not covered by UDAP statutes.

Where the conditions for fraud are met, as they are in many common scams and one-on-one deceptive practices, a UDAP violation will almost

---

[106]   *See* CAL. CIV. CODE § 1780(a) (West 2003); CONN. GEN. STAT. § 42-110(a) (2003); GA. CODE ANN. 10-1-399(a) (2003); IDAHO CODE §§ 48-608(1), (4) (2003); KY. REV. STAT. § 367.220(1) (Michie 2003); MO. REV. STAT. § 407.025.1 (2003); ORE. REV. STAT. § 646.638(1) (2001); R.I. GEN. LAWS § 6-13.1-5.2(c) (2002).

[107]   *See* FLA. STAT. ANN. § 501.211(2) (2003) (but Florida does mandatorily award costs and fees to the prevailing party, Fla. Stat. Ann. § 501.2105(1)); 815 ILL. COMP. STAT. 505/10a (2003); Martin v. Heinold Commodities, Inc., 643 N.E.2d 734 (Ill. 1994); IND. CODE. ANN. § 24-5-0.5-4(a) (2003); KAN. STAT. ANN. § 50-634 (2002); ME. REV. STAT. ANN. tit. 5, § 213.1 (West 2003); MD. CODE ANN., COM. LAW I § 13-408(a) (2003); MICH. STAT. ANN. § 19.418(11)(1) (2003); MINN. STAT. § 8.31 (2003); MISS. CODE ANN. § 75-24-15(1) (2003); NEB. REV. STAT. § 59-1609 (2003); NEV. REV. STAT. § 41.600; OKLA. STAT. tit. 15, § 761.1a (2002) ; S.D. CODIFIED LAWS ANN. § 37-24-31 (Michie 2003); UTAH CODE ANN. § 13-11-19 (2003) (but imposes minimum relief of $2,000 plus costs); VA. CODE ANN. § 59.1-204 (2003) (but imposes minimum relief of $100); W. VA. CODE § 46A-6-106 (2003) (but imposes minimum relief of $200); WIS. STAT. § 100.18(11)(b)(2) (2003); WYO. STAT. § 40-12-108(a) (2002).

always also be found if the statute reaches the relevant transaction. A consumer-plaintiff may find that the punitive recovery for fraud far exceeds the actual damages awarded under the UDAP statute, even if the circumstances warrant a statutory multiplication of damages. Accordingly, consumers are almost always well advised to add a fraud claim to their UDAP actions where the conditions of intentional deception and demonstrable injury are present.

EXCERPTS OF IMPORTANT FEDERAL, UNIFORM, AND STATE CONSUMER PROTECTION STATUTES

1. Section 5 of the Federal Trade Commission Act, 15 U.S.C. § 45

Sec. 45. - Unfair methods of competition unlawful; prevention by Commission

(a) Declaration of unlawfulness; power to prohibit unfair practices; inapplicability to foreign trade

(1) Unfair methods of competition in or affecting commerce, and unfair or deceptive acts or practices in or affecting commerce, are hereby declared unlawful.

(2) The Commission is hereby empowered and directed to prevent persons, partnerships, or corporations, except banks, savings and loan institutions described in section 57a(f)(3) of this title, Federal credit unions described in section 57a(f)(4) of this title, common carriers subject to the Acts to regulate commerce, air carriers and foreign air carriers subject to part A of subtitle VII of title 49, and persons, partnerships, or corporations insofar as they are subject to the Packers and Stockyards Act, 1921, as amended (7 U.S.C. 181 et seq.), except as provided in section 406(b) of said Act (7 U.S.C. 227(b)), from using unfair methods of competition in or affecting commerce and unfair or deceptive acts or practices in or affecting commerce.

(3) This subsection shall not apply to unfair methods of competition involving commerce with foreign nations (other than import commerce) unless -

(A) such methods of competition have a direct, substantial, and reasonably foreseeable effect -

(i) on commerce which is not commerce with foreign nations, or on import commerce with foreign nations; or

(ii) on export commerce with foreign nations, of a person engaged in such commerce in the United States; and

(B) such effect gives rise to a claim under the provisions of this subsection, other than this paragraph.

If this subsection applies to such methods of competition only because of the operation of subparagraph (A)(ii), this subsection shall apply to such conduct only for injury to export business in the United States.

(b) Proceeding by Commission; modifying and setting aside orders

Whenever the Commission shall have reason to believe that any such person, partnership, or corporation has been or is using any unfair method of competition or unfair or deceptive act or practice in or affecting commerce, and if it shall appear to the Commission that a proceeding by it in respect thereof would be to the interest of the public, it shall issue and serve upon such person, partnership, or corporation a complaint stating its charges in that respect and containing a notice of a hearing upon a day and at a place therein fixed at least thirty days after the service of said complaint. The person, partnership, or corporation so complained of shall have the right to appear at the place and time so fixed and show cause why an order should not be entered by the Commission requiring such person, partnership, or corporation to cease and desist from the violation of the law so charged in said complaint. Any person, partnership, or corporation may make application, and upon good cause shown may be allowed by the Commission to intervene and appear in said proceeding by counsel or in person. The testimony in any such proceeding shall be reduced to writing and filed in the office of the Commission. If upon such hearing the Commission shall be of the opinion that the method of competition or the act or practice in question is prohibited by this subchapter, it shall make a report in writing in which it shall state its findings as to the facts and shall issue and cause to be served on such person, partnership, or corporation an order requiring such person, partnership, or corporation to cease and desist from using such method of competition or such act or practice. Until the expiration of the time allowed for filing a petition for review, if no such petition has been duly filed within such time, or, if a petition for review has been filed within such time then until the record in the proceeding has been filed in a court of appeals of the United States, as hereinafter provided, the Commission may at any time, upon such notice and in such manner as it shall deem proper, modify or set aside, in whole or in part, any report or any order made or issued by it under this section. After the expiration of the time allowed for filing a petition for review, if no such petition has been duly filed within such time, the Commission may at any time, after notice and opportunity for hearing, reopen and alter, modify, or set aside, in whole or in part any report or order made or issued by it under this section, whenever in the opinion of the Commission conditions of fact or of law have so changed as to require such action or if the public interest shall so require, except that

(1) the said person, partnership, or corporation may, within sixty days after service upon him or it of said report or order entered after such a reopening, obtain a review thereof in the appropriate court of appeals of the United States, in the manner provided in subsection (c) of this section; and

(2) in the case of an order, the Commission shall reopen any such order to consider whether such order (including any affirmative relief provision contained in such order) should be altered, modified, or set aside, in whole or in part, if the person, partnership, or corporation involved files a request with the Commission which makes a satisfactory showing that changed conditions of law or fact require such order to be altered, modified, or set aside, in whole or in part. The Commission shall determine whether to alter, modify, or set aside any order of the Commission in response to a request made by a person, partnership, or corporation under paragraph (2) not later than 120 days after the date of the filing of such request.

(c) Review of order; rehearing

Any person, partnership, or corporation required by an order of the Commission to cease and desist from using any method of competition or act or practice may obtain a review of such order in the court of appeals of the United States, within any circuit where the method of competition or the act or practice in question was used or where such person, partnership, or corporation resides or carries on business, by filing in the court, within sixty days from the date of the service of such order, a written petition praying that the order of the Commission be set aside. A copy of such petition shall be forthwith transmitted by the clerk of the court to the Commission, and thereupon the Commission shall file in the court the record in the proceeding, as provided in section 2112 of title 28. Upon such filing of the petition the court shall have jurisdiction of the proceeding and of the question determined therein concurrently with the Commission until the filing of the record and shall have power to make and enter a decree affirming, modifying, or setting aside the order of the Commission, and enforcing the same to the extent that such order is affirmed and to issue such writs as are ancillary to its jurisdiction or are necessary in its judgement to prevent injury to the public or to competitors pendente lite. The findings of the Commission as to the facts, if supported by evidence, shall be conclusive. To the extent that the order of the Commission is affirmed, the court shall thereupon issue its own order commanding obedience to the terms of such order of the Commission. If either party shall apply to the court for leave to adduce additional evidence, and shall show to the satisfaction of the court that such additional evidence is material and that there were reasonable grounds for the failure to adduce such evidence in the proceeding before the Commission, the court may order such additional evidence to be taken before the Commission and to be adduced upon the hearing in such manner and upon such terms and conditions as to the court may seem proper. The Commission may modify its findings as to the facts, or make new findings, by reason of the additional evidence so taken, and it shall file such modified or new findings, which, if supported by evidence, shall be conclusive, and its recommendation, if any, for the modification or setting aside of its original order, with the return of such additional evidence. The judgment and decree of the court shall be final, except that the same shall be subject to review by the Supreme Court upon certiorari, as provided in section 1254 of title 28.

(d) Jurisdiction of court

Upon the filing of the record with it the jurisdiction of the court of appeals of the United States to affirm, enforce, modify, or set aside orders of the Commission shall be exclusive.

(e) Exemption from liability

No order of the Commission or judgement of court to enforce the same shall in anywise relieve or absolve any person, partnership, or corporation from any liability under the Antitrust Acts.

(f) Service of complaints, orders and other processes; return

Complaints, orders, and other processes of the Commission under this section may be served by anyone duly authorized by the Commission, either

(a) by delivering a copy thereof to the person to be served, or to a member of the partnership to be served, or the president, secretary, or other executive officer or a director of the corporation to be served; or

(b) by leaving a copy thereof at the residence or the principal office or place of business of such person, partnership, or corporation; or

(c) by mailing a copy thereof by registered mail or by certified mail addressed to such person, partnership, or corporation at his or its residence or principal office or place of business. The verified return by the person so serving said complaint, order, or other process setting forth the manner of said service shall be proof of the same, and the return post office receipt for said complaint, order, or other process mailed by registered mail or by certified mail as aforesaid shall be proof of the service of the same.

(g) Finality of order

An order of the Commission to cease and desist shall become final -

(1) Upon the expiration of the time allowed for filing a petition for review, if no such petition has been duly filed within such time; but the Commission may thereafter modify or set aside its order to the extent provided in the last sentence of subsection (b).

(2) Except as to any order provision subject to paragraph (4), upon the sixtieth day after such order is served, if a petition for review has been duly filed; except that any such order may be stayed, in whole or in part and subject to such conditions as may be appropriate, by -

(A) the Commission;

(B) an appropriate court of appeals of the United States, if

(i) a petition for review of such order is pending in such court, and

(ii) an application for such a stay was previously submitted to the Commission and the Commission, within the 30-day period beginning on the date the application was received by the Commission, either denied the application or did not grant or deny the application; or

(C) the Supreme Court, if an applicable petition for certiorari is pending.

(3) For purposes of subsection (m)(1)(B) of this section and of section 57b(a)(2) of this title, if a petition for review of the order of the Commission has been filed -

(A) upon the expiration of the time allowed for filing a petition for certiorari, if the order of the Commission has been affirmed or the petition for review has been dismissed by the court of appeals and no petition for certiorari has been duly filed;

(B) upon the denial of a petition for certiorari, if the order of the Commission has been affirmed or the petition for review has been dismissed by the court of appeals; or

(C) upon the expiration of 30 days from the date of issuance of a mandate of the Supreme Court directing that the order of the Commission be affirmed or the petition for review be dismissed.

(4) In the case of an order provision requiring a person, partnership, or corporation to divest itself of stock, other share

capital, or assets, if a petition for review of such order of the Commission has been filed -

(A) upon the expiration of the time allowed for filing a petition for certiorari, if the order of the Commission has been affirmed or the petition for review has been dismissed by the court of appeals and no petition for certiorari has been duly filed;

(B) upon the denial of a petition for certiorari, if the order of the Commission has been affirmed or the petition for review has been dismissed by the court of appeals; or

(C) upon the expiration of 30 days from the date of issuance of a mandate of the Supreme Court directing that the order of the Commission be affirmed or the petition for review be dismissed.

(h) Modification or setting aside of order by Supreme Court

If the Supreme Court directs that the order of the Commission be modified or set aside, the order of the Commission rendered in accordance with the mandate of the Supreme Court shall become final upon the expiration of thirty days from the time it was rendered, unless within such thirty days either party has instituted proceedings to have such order corrected to accord with the mandate, in which event the order of the Commission shall become final when so corrected.

(i) Modification or setting aside of order by Court of Appeals

If the order of the Commission is modified or set aside by the court of appeals, and if

(1) the time allowed for filing a petition for certiorari has expired and no such petition has been duly filed, or

(2) the petition for certiorari has been denied, or

(3) the decision of the court has been affirmed by the Supreme Court, then the order of the Commission rendered in accordance with the mandate of the court of appeals shall become final on the expiration of thirty days from the time such order of the Commission was rendered, unless within such thirty days either party has instituted proceedings to have such order corrected so that it will accord with the mandate, in which event the order of the Commission shall become final when so corrected.

(j) Rehearing upon order or remand

If the Supreme Court orders a rehearing; or if the case is remanded by the court of appeals to the Commission for a rehearing, and if

(1) the time allowed for filing a petition for certiorari has expired, and no such petition has been duly filed, or

(2) the petition for certiorari has been denied, or

(3) the decision of the court has been affirmed by the Supreme Court, then the order of the Commission rendered upon such rehearing shall become final in the same manner as though no prior order of the Commission had been rendered.

(k) "Mandate" defined

As used in this section the term "mandate", in case a mandate has been recalled prior to the expiration of thirty days from the date of issuance thereof, means the final mandate.

(l) Penalty for violation of order; injunctions and other appropriate equitable relief

Any person, partnership, or corporation who violates an order of the Commission after it has become final, and while such order is in effect, shall forfeit and pay to the United States a civil penalty of not more than $10,000 for each violation, which shall accrue to the United States and may be recovered in a civil action brought by the Attorney General of the United States. Each separate violation of such an order shall be a separate offense, except that in a case of a violation through continuing failure to obey or neglect to obey a final order of the Commission, each day of continuance of such failure or neglect shall be deemed a separate offense. In such actions, the United States district courts are empowered to grant mandatory injunctions and such other and further equitable relief as they deem appropriate in the enforcement of such final orders of the Commission.

(m) Civil actions for recovery of penalties for knowing violations of rules and cease and desist orders respecting unfair or deceptive acts or practices; jurisdiction; maximum amount of penalties; continuing violations; de novo determinations; compromise or settlement procedure

(1)

(A) The Commission may commence a civil action to recover a civil penalty in a district court of the United States against any person, partnership, or corporation which violates any rule under this chapter respecting unfair or deceptive acts or practices (other than an interpretive rule or a rule violation of which the Commission has provided is not an unfair or deceptive act or practice in violation of subsection (a)(1) of this section) with actual knowledge or knowledge fairly implied on the basis of objective circumstances that such act is unfair or deceptive and is prohibited by such rule. In such action, such person, partnership, or corporation shall be liable for a civil penalty of not more than $10,000 for each violation.

(B) If the Commission determines in a proceeding under subsection (b) of this section that any act or practice is unfair or deceptive, and issues a final cease and desist order, other than a consent order, with respect to such act or practice, then the Commission may commence a civil action to obtain a civil penalty in a district court of the United States against any person, partnership, or corporation which engages in such act or practice -

(1) after such cease and desist order becomes final (whether or not such person, partnership, or corporation was subject to such cease and desist order), and

(2) with actual knowledge that such act or practice is unfair or deceptive and is unlawful under subsection (a)(1) of this section.

In such action, such person, partnership, or corporation shall be liable for a civil penalty of not more than $10,000 for each violation.

(C) In the case of a violation through continuing failure to comply with a rule or with subsection (a)(1) of this section, each day of continuance of such failure shall be treated as a separate violation, for purposes of subparagraphs (A) and (B). In determining the amount of such a civil penalty, the court shall take into account the degree of culpability, any history of prior such conduct, ability to pay, effect on ability to continue to do business, and such other matters as justice may require.

(2) If the cease and desist order establishing that the act or practice is unfair or deceptive was not issued against the defendant in a civil penalty action under paragraph (1)(B) the issues of fact in such action against such defendant shall be tried de novo. Upon request of any party to such an action against such defendant, the court shall also review the determination of law made by the Commission in the proceeding under subsection (b) of this section that the act or practice which was the subject of such proceeding constituted an unfair or deceptive act or practice in violation of subsection (a) of this section.

(3) The Commission may compromise or settle any action for a civil penalty if such compromise or settlement is accompanied by a public statement of its reasons and is approved by the court.

(n) Standard of proof; public policy consideration

The Commission shall have no authority under this section or section[1] of this title to declare unlawful an act or practice on the grounds that such act or practice is unfair unless the act or practice causes or is likely to cause substantial injury to consumers which is not reasonably avoidable by consumers themselves and not outweighed by countervailing benefits to consumers or to competition. In determining whether an act or practice is unfair, the Commission may consider established public policies as evidence to be considered with all other evidence. Such public policy considerations may not serve as a primary basis for such determination

---

[1]   The repetition of "section" is usually interpreted as a typographical error that should read, "section or clause".

2. Sections 34(a), 35(a), and 43(a) of the Lanham Act (15 U.S.C. §§ 1116(a), 1117(a), 1125(a))

§1116. Injunctive relief

(a) Jurisdiction; service

The several courts vested with jurisdiction of civil actions arising under this chapter shall have power to grant injunctions, according to the principles of equity and upon such terms as the court may deem reasonable, to prevent the violation of any right of the registrant of a mark registered in the Patent and Trademark Office or to prevent a violation under subsection (a), (c), or (d) of section 1125 of this title. Any such injunction may include a provision directing the defendant to file with the court and serve on the plaintiff within thirty days after the service on the defendant of such injunction, or such extended period as the court may direct, a report in writing under oath setting forth in detail the manner and form in which the defendant has complied with the injunction. Any such injunction granted upon hearing, after notice to the defendant, by any district court of the United States, may be served on the parties against whom such injunction is granted anywhere in the United States where they may be found, and shall be operative and may be enforced by proceedings to punish for contempt, or otherwise, by the court by which such injunction was granted, or by any other United States district court in whose jurisdiction the defendant may be found.

§1117. Recovery for violation of rights

(a) Profits; damages and costs; attorney fees

When a violation of any right of the registrant of a mark registered in the Patent and Trademark Office, a violation under section 1125(a), (c), or (d) of this title, or a willful violation under section 1125(c) of this title, shall have been established in any civil action arising under this chapter, the plaintiff shall be entitled, subject to the provisions of sections 1111 and 1114 of this title, and subject to the principles of equity, to recover

(1) defendant's profits,

(2) any damages sustained by the plaintiff, and

(3) the costs of the action.

The court shall assess such profits and damages or cause the same to be assessed under its direction. In assessing profits the plaintiff shall be required to prove defendant's sales only; defendant must prove all elements of cost or deduction claimed. In assessing damages the court may enter judgment, according to the circumstances of the case, for any sum above the amount found as actual damages, not exceeding three times such amount. If the court shall find that the amount of the recovery based on profits is either inadequate or excessive the court may in its discretion enter judgment for such sum as the court shall find to be just, according to the circumstances of the case. Such sum in either of the above circumstances shall constitute compensation and not a penalty. The court in exceptional cases may award reasonable attorney fees to the prevailing party.

* * *

§1125. False designations of origin and false descriptions forbidden

(a) Civil action.

(1) Any person who, on or in connection with any goods or services, or any container for goods, uses in commerce any word, term, name, symbol, or device, or any combination thereof, or any false designation of origin, false or misleading description of fact, or false or misleading representation of fact, which--

(A) is likely to cause confusion, or to cause mistake, or to deceive as to the affiliation, connection, or association of such person with another person, or as to the origin, sponsorship, or approval of his or her goods, services, or commercial activities by another person, or

(B) in commercial advertising or promotion, misrepresents the nature, characteristics, qualities, or geographic origin of his or her or another person's goods, services, or commercial activities, shall be liable in a civil action by any person who believes that he or she is or is likely to be damaged by such act.

(2) As used in this subsection, the term "any person" includes any State, instrumentality of a State or employee of a State or instrumentality of a State acting in his or her official capacity. Any State, and any such instrumentality, officer, or employee, shall be subject to the provisions of this Act in the same manner and to the same extent as any nongovernmental entity.

(3) In a civil action for trade dress infringement under this Act for trade dress not registered on the principal register, the person who asserts trade dress protection has the burden of proving that the matter sought to be protected is not functional.

3. *Sections 1 to 7 of The Uniform Deceptive Trade Practices Act*

SECTION 1. [Definitions.] As used in this Act, unless the context otherwise requires:

(1) "article" means a product as distinguished from its trademark, label, ordistinctive dress in packaging;

(2) "certification mark" means a mark used in connection with the goods or services of a person other than the certifier to indicate geographic origin, material, mode of manufacture, quality, accuracy, or other characteristics of the goods or services or to indicate that the work or labor on the goods or services was performed by members of a union or other organization;

(3) "collective mark" means a mark used by members of a cooperative, association, or other collective group or organization to identify goods or services and distinguish them from those of others, or to indicate membership in the collective group or organization;

(4) "mark" means a word, name, symbol, device, or any combination of the foregoing in any form or arrangement;

(5) "person" means an individual, corporation, government, or governmental subdivision or agency, business trust, estate, trust, partnership, unincorporated association, two or more of any of the foregoing having a joint or common interest, or any other legal or commercial entity;

(6) "service mark" means a mark used by a person to identify services and to distinguish them from the services of others;

(7) "trademark" means a mark used by a person to identify goods and to distinguish them from the goods of others;

(8) "trade name" means a word, name, symbol, device, or any combination of the foregoing in any form or arrangement used by a person to identify his business, vocation, or occupation and distinguish it from the business, vocation, or occupation of others.

SECTION 2. [Deceptive Trade Practices.]

(a) A person engages in a deceptive trade practice when, in the course of his business, vocation, or occupation, he:

(1) passes off goods or services as those of another;

(2) causes likelihood of confusion or of misunderstanding as to the source, sponsorship, approval, or certification of goods or services;

(3) causes likelihood of confusion or of misunderstanding as to affiliation, connection, or association with, or certification by, another;

(4) uses deceptive representations or designations of geographic origin in connection with goods or services;

(5) represents that goods or services have sponsorship, approval, characteristics, ingredients, uses, benefits, or quantities that they do not have or that a person has a sponsorship, approval, status, affiliation, or connection that he does not have;

(6) represents that goods are original or new if they are deteriorated, altered, reconditioned, reclaimed, used, or second-hand;

(7) represents that goods or services are of a particular standard, quality, or grade, or that goods are of a particular style or model, if they are of another;

(8) disparages the goods, services, or business of another by false or misleading representation of fact;

(9) advertises goods or services with intent not to sell them as advertised;

(10) advertises goods or services with intent not to supply reasonably expectable public demand, unless the advertisement discloses a limitation of quantity;

(11) makes false or misleading statements of fact concerning the reasons for, existence of, or amounts of price reductions; or

(12) engages in any other conduct which similarly creates a likelihood of confusion or of misunderstanding.

(b) In order to prevail in an action under this Act, a complainant need not prove competition between the parties or actual confusion or misunderstanding.

(c) This section does not affect unfair trade practices otherwise actionable at common law or under other statutes of this state.

SECTION 3. [Remedies.]

(a) A person likely to be damaged by a deceptive trade practice of another may be granted an injunction against it under the principles of equity and on terms that the court considers reasonable. Proof of monetary damage, loss of profits, or intent to deceive is not required. Relief granted for the copying of an article shall be limited to the prevention of confusion or misunderstanding as to source.

(b) Costs shall be allowed to the prevailing party unless the court otherwise directs. The court [in its discretion] may award attorneys' fees to the prevailing party if (1) the party complaining of a deceptive trade practice has brought an action which he knew to be groundless or (2) the party charged with a deceptive trade practice has willfully engaged in the trade practice knowing it to be deceptive.

(c) The relief provided in this section is in addition to remedies otherwise available against the same conduct under the common law or other statutes of this state.

SECTION 4. [Application.]

(a) This Act does not apply to:

(1) conduct in compliance with the orders or rules of, or a statute administered by, a federal, state, or local governmental agency;

(2) publishers, broadcasters, printers, or other persons engaged in the dissemination of information or reproduction of printed or pictorial matters who publish, broadcast, or reproduce material without knowledge of its deceptive character; or

(3) actions or appeals pending on the effective date of this Act.

(b) Subsections 2(a)(2) and 2(a)(3) do not apply to the use of a service mark, trademark, certification mark, collective mark, trade name, or other trade identification that was used and not abandoned before the effective date of this Act, if the use was in good faith and is otherwise lawful except for this Act.

SECTION 5. [Uniformity of Interpretation.] This Act shall be construed to effectuate its general purpose to make uniform the law of those states which enact it.

SECTION 6. [Short Title.] This Act may be cited as the Uniform Deceptive Trade Practices Act.

SECTION 7. [Severability.] If any provision of this Act or the application thereof to any person or circumstance is held invalid, the invalidity does not affect other provisions or applications of the Act which can be given effect without the invalid provision or application, and to this end the provisions of this Act are severable.

4. ***Massachusetts M.G.L. ch. 93A (An Example of a State "Little FTC Act")***

CHAPTER 93A. REGULATION OF BUSINESS PRACTICES FOR CONSUMERS PROTECTION.
Chapter 93A: Section 1. Definitions.
Section 1. The following words, as used in this chapter unless the text otherwise requires or a different meaning is specifically required, shall mean:-

(a) "Person" shall include, where applicable, natural persons, corporations, trusts, partnerships, incorporated or unincorporated associations, and any other legal entity.

(b) "Trade" and ""commerce" shall include the advertising, the offering for sale, rent or lease, the sale, rent, lease or distribution of any services and any property, tangible or intangible, real, personal or mixed, any security as defined in subparagraph (k) of section four hundred and one of chapter one hundred and ten A and any contract of sale of a commodity for future delivery, and any other article, commodity, or thing of value wherever situate, and shall include any trade or commerce directly or indirectly affecting the people of this commonwealth.

(c) "Documentary material" shall include the original or a copy of any book, record, report, memorandum, paper, communication, tabulation, map, chart, photograph, mechanical transcription, or other tangible document or recording, wherever situate.

(d) "Examination of documentary material", the inspection, study, or copying of any such material, and the taking of testimony under oath or acknowledgment in respect of any such documentary material.
Chapter 93A: Section 2. Unfair practices; legislative intent; rules and regulations.
Section 2.

(a) Unfair methods of competition and unfair or deceptive acts or practices in the conduct of any trade or commerce are hereby declared unlawful.

(b) It is the intent of the legislature that in construing paragraph (a) of this section in actions brought under sections four, nine and eleven, the courts will be guided by the interpretations given by the Federal Trade Commission and the Federal Courts to section 5(a)(1) of the Federal Trade Commission Act (15 U.S.C. 45(a)(1)), as from time to time amended.

(c) The attorney general may make rules and regulations interpreting the provisions of subsection 2(a) of this chapter. Such rules and regulations shall not be inconsistent with the rules, regulations and decisions of the Federal Trade Commission and the Federal Courts interpreting the provisions of 15 U.S.C. 45(a)(1) (The Federal Trade Commission Act), as from time to time amended.

Chapter 93A: Section 3. Exempted transactions.

Section 3. Nothing in this chapter shall apply to transactions or actions otherwise permitted under laws as administered by any regulatory board or officer acting under statutory authority of the commonwealth or of the United States.

For the purpose of this section, the burden of proving exemptions from the provisions of this chapter shall be upon the person claiming the exemptions.

Chapter 93A: Section 4. Actions by attorney general; notice; venue; injunctions.

Section 4. Whenever the attorney general has reason to believe that any person is using or is about to use any method, act, or practice declared by section two to be unlawful, and that proceedings would be in the public interest, he may bring an action in the name of the commonwealth against such person to restrain by temporary restraining order or preliminary or permanent injunction the use of such method, act or practice. The action may be brought in the superior court of the county in which such person resides or has his principal place of business, or the action may be brought in the superior court of Suffolk county with the consent of the parties or if the person has no place of business within the commonwealth. If more than one person is joined as a defendant, such action may be brought in the superior court of the county where any one defendant resides or has his principal place of business, or in Suffolk county. Said court may issue temporary restraining orders or preliminary or permanent injunctions and make such other orders or judgments as may be necessary to restore to any person who has suffered any ascertainable loss by reason of the use or employment of such unlawful method, act or practice any moneys or property, real or personal, which may have been acquired by means of such method, act, or practice. If the court finds that a person has employed any method, act or practice which he knew or should have known to be in violation of said section two, the court may require such person to pay to the commonwealth a civil penalty of not more than five thousand dollars for each such violation and also may require the said person to pay the reasonable costs of investigation and litigation of such violation, including reasonable attorneys' fees. If the court finds any method, act, or practice unlawful with regard to any security or any contract of sale of a commodity for future delivery as defined in section two, the court may issue such orders or judgments as may be necessary to restore any person who has suffered any ascertainable loss of any moneys or property, real or personal, or up to three but not less than two times that amount if the court finds that the use of the act or practice was a willful violation of said section two, a civil penalty to be paid to the commonwealth of not more than five thousand dollars for each such violation, and also may require said person to pay the reasonable costs of investigation and litigation of such violation, including reasonable attorneys fees.

At least five days prior to the commencement of any action brought under this section, except when a temporary restraining order is sought, the attorney general shall notify the person of his intended action, and give the person an opportunity to confer with the attorney general in person or by counsel or other representative as to the proposed action. Such notice shall be given the person by mail, postage prepaid, to his usual place of business, or if he has no usual place of business, to his last known address.

Any district attorney or law enforcement officer receiving notice of any alleged violation of this chapter or of any violation of an injunction or order issued in an action brought under this section shall immediately forward written notice of the same together with any information that he may have to the office of the attorney general.

Any person who violates the terms of an injunction or other order issued under this section shall forfeit and pay to the commonwealth a civil penalty of not more than ten thousand dollars for each violation. For the purposes of this section, the court issuing such an injunction or order shall retain jurisdiction, and the cause shall be continued, and in such case the attorney general acting in the name of the commonwealth may petition for recovery of such civil penalty.

Chapter 93A: Section 5. Assurance of discontinuance of unlawful method or practice.

Section 5. In any case where the attorney general has authority to institute an action or proceeding under section four, in lieu thereof he may accept an assurance of discontinuance of any method, act or practice in violation of this chapter from any person alleged to be engaged or to have been engaged in such method, act or practice. Such assurance may, among other terms, include a stipulation for the voluntary payment by such person of the costs of investigation, or of an amount to be held in escrow pending the outcome of an action or as restitution to aggrieved buyers, or both. Any such assurance of discontinuance shall be in writing and be filed with the superior court of Suffolk county. Matters thus closed may at any time be reopened by the attorney general for further proceedings in the public interest. Evidence of a violation of such assurance shall be prima facie evidence of a violation of section two in any subsequent proceeding brought by the attorney general.

Chapter 93A: Section 6. Examination of books and records; attendance of persons; notice.

Section 6.

(1) The attorney general, whenever he believes a person has engaged in or is engaging in any method, act or practice declared to be unlawful by this chapter, may conduct an investigation to ascertain whether in fact such person has engaged in or is engaging in such method, act or practice. In conducting such investigation he may (a) take testimony under oath concerning such alleged unlawful method, act or practice; (b) examine or cause to be examined any documentary material of whatever nature relevant to such alleged unlawful method, act or practice; and (c) require attendance during such examination of documentary material of any person having knowledge of the documentary material and take testimony under oath or acknowledgment in respect of any such documentary material. Such testimony and examination shall take place in the county where such person resides or has a place of business or, if the parties consent or such person is a nonresident or has no place of business within the commonwealth, in Suffolk county.

(2) Notice of the time, place and cause of such taking of testimony, examination or attendance shall be given by the attorney general at least ten days prior to the date of such taking of testimony or examination.

(3) Service of any such notice may be made by (a) delivering a duly executed copy thereof to the person to be served or to a partner or to any officer or agent authorized by appointment or by law to receive service of process on behalf of such person; (b) delivering a duly executed copy thereof to the principal place of business in the commonwealth of the person to be served; or (c) mailing by registered or certified mail a duly executed copy thereof addressed to the person to be served at the principal place of business in the commonwealth or, if said person has no place of business in the commonwealth, to his principal office or place of business.

(4) Each such notice shall (a) state the time and place for the taking of testimony or the examination and the name and address of each person to be examined, if known, and, if the name is not known, a general description sufficient to identify him or the particular class or group to which he belongs; (b) state the statute and section thereof, the alleged violation of which is under investigation and the general subject matter of the investigation; (c) describe the class of classes of documentary material to be produced thereunder with reasonable specificity, so as fairly to indicate the material demanded; (d) prescribe a return date within which the documentary material is to

be produced; and (e) identify the members of the attorney general's staff to whom such documentary material is to be made available for inspection and copying.

(5) No such notice shall contain any requirement which would be unreasonable or improper if contained in a subpoena duces tecum issued by a court of the commonwealth; or require the disclosure of any documentary material which would be privileged, or which for any other reason would not be required by a subpoena duces tecum issued by a court of the commonwealth.

(6) Any documentary material or other information produced by any person pursuant to this section shall not, unless otherwise ordered by a court of the commonwealth for good cause shown, be disclosed to any person other than the authorized agent or representative of the attorney general, unless with the consent of the person producing the same; provided, however, that such material or information may be disclosed by the attorney general in court pleadings or other papers filed in court.

(7) At any time prior to the date specified in the notice, or within twenty-one days after the notice has been served, whichever period is shorter, the court may, upon motion for good cause shown, extend such reporting date or modify or set aside such demand or grant a protective order in accordance with the standards set forth in Rule 26(c) of the Massachusetts Rules of Civil Procedure. The motion may be filed in the superior court of the county in which the person served resides or has his usual place of business, or in Suffolk county. This section shall not be applicable to any criminal proceeding nor shall information obtained under the authority of this section be admissible in evidence in any criminal prosecution for substantially identical transactions.

Chapter 93A: Section 7. Failure to appear or to comply with notice.

Section 7. A person upon whom a notice is served pursuant to the provisions of section six shall comply with the terms thereof unless otherwise provided by the order of a court of the commonwealth. Any person who fails to appear, or with intent to avoid, evade, or prevent compliance, in whole or in part, with any civil investigation under this chapter, removes from any place, conceals, withholds, or destroys, mutilates, alters, or by any other means falsifies any documentary material in the possession, custody or control of any person subject to any such notice, or knowingly conceals any relevant information, shall be assessed a civil penalty of not more than five thousand dollars.

The attorney general may file in **the** superior court of the county in which such person resides or has his principal place of business, or of Suffolk county if such person is a nonresident or has no principal place of business in the commonwealth, and serve upon such person, in the same manner as provided in section six, a petition for an order of such court for the enforcement of this section and section six. Any disobedience of any final order entered under this section by any court shall be punished as a contempt thereof.

Chapter 93A: Section 8. Habitual violation of injunctions.

Section 8. Upon petition by the attorney general, the court may for habitual violation of injunctions issued pursuant to section four order the dissolution, or suspension or forfeiture of franchise of any corporation or the right of any individual or foreign corporation to do business in the commonwealth.

Chapter 93A: Section 9. Civil actions and remedies; class action; demand for relief; damages; costs; exhausting administrative remedies.

Section 9.

(1) Any person, other than a person entitled to bring action under section eleven of this chapter, who has been injured by another person's use or employment of any method, act or practice declared to be unlawful by section two or any rule or regulation issued thereunder or any person whose rights are affected by another person violating the provisions of clause (9) of section three of chapter one hundred and seventy-six D may bring an action in the superior court, or in the housing court as provided in section three of chapter one hundred and eighty-five C whether by way of original complaint, counterclaim, cross-claim or third party action, for damages and such equitable relief, including an injunction, as the court deems to be necessary and proper.

(2) Any persons entitled to bring such action may, if the use or employment of the unfair or deceptive act or practice has caused similar injury to numerous other persons similarly situated and if the court finds in a preliminary hearing that he adequately and fairly represents such other persons, bring the action on behalf of himself and such other similarly injured and situated persons; the court shall require that notice of such action be given to unnamed petitioners in the most effective practicable manner. Such action shall not be dismissed, settled or compromised without the approval of the court, and notice of any proposed dismissal, settlement or compromise shall be given to all members of the class of petitioners in such manner as the court directs.

(3) At least thirty days prior to the filing of any such action, a written demand for relief, identifying the claimant and reasonably describing the unfair or deceptive act or practice relied upon and the injury suffered, shall be mailed or delivered to any prospective respondent.

Any person receiving such a demand for relief who, within thirty days of the mailing or delivery of the demand for relief, makes a written tender of settlement which is rejected by the claimant may, in any subsequent action, file the written tender and an affidavit concerning its rejection and thereby limit any recovery to the relief tendered if the court finds that the relief tendered was reasonable in relation to the injury actually suffered by the petitioner. In all other cases, if the court finds for the petitioner, recovery shall be in the amount of actual damages or twenty-five dollars, whichever is greater; or up to three but not less than two times such amount if the court finds that the use or employment of the act or practice was a willful or knowing violation of said section two or that the refusal to grant relief upon demand was made in bad faith with knowledge or reason to know that the act or practice complained of violated said section two. For the purposes of this chapter, the amount of actual damages to be multiplied by the court shall be the amount of the judgment on all claims arising out of the same and underlying transaction or occurrence, regardless of the existence or nonexistence of insurance coverage available in payment of the claim. In addition, the court shall award such other equitable relief, including an injunction, as it deems to be necessary and proper. The demand requirements of this paragraph shall not apply if the claim is asserted by way of counterclaim or cross-claim, or if the prospective respondent does not maintain a place of business or does not keep assets within the commonwealth, but such respondent may otherwise employ the provisions of this section by making a written offer of relief and paying the rejected tender into court as soon as practicable after receiving notice of an action commenced under this section. Notwithstanding any other provision to the contrary, if the court finds any method, act or practice unlawful with regard to any security or any contract of sale of a commodity for future delivery as defined in section two, and if the court finds for the petitioner, recovery shall be in the amount of actual damages.

(3A) A person may assert a claim under this section in a district court, whether by way of original complaint, counterclaim, cross-claim or third-party action, for money damages only. Said damages may include double or treble damages, attorneys' fees and costs, as herein provided. The demand requirements and provision for tender of offer of settlement provided in paragraph (3) shall also be applicable under this paragraph, except that no rights to equitable relief shall be created under this paragraph, nor shall a person asserting a claim hereunder be able to assert any claim on behalf of other similarly insured and situated persons as provided in paragraph

(2). The provisions of sections ninety-five to one hundred and ten, inclusive, of chapter two hundred and thirty-one, where applicable, shall apply to a claim under this section, except that the provisions for remand, removal and transfer shall be controlled by the amount of single damages claimed hereunder.

(4) If the court finds in any action commenced hereunder that there has been a violation of section two, the petitioner shall, in addition to other relief provided for by this section and irrespective of the amount in controversy, be awarded reasonable attorney's fees and costs incurred in connection with said action; provided, however, the court shall deny recovery of attorney's fees and costs which are incurred after the rejection of a reasonable written offer of settlement made within thirty days of the mailing or delivery of the written demand for relief required by this section.

[There is no paragraph (5).]

(6) Any person entitled to bring an action under this section shall not be required to initiate, pursue or exhaust any remedy established by any regulation, administrative procedure, local, state or federal law or statute or the common law in order to bring an action under this section or to obtain injunctive relief or recover damages or attorney's fees or costs or other relief as provided in this section. Failure to exhaust administrative remedies shall not be a defense to any proceeding under this section, except as provided in paragraph seven.

(7) The court may upon motion by the respondent before the time for answering and after a hearing suspend proceedings brought under this section to permit the respondent to initiate action in which the petitioner shall be named a party before any appropriate regulatory board or officer providing adjudicatory hearings to complainants if the respondent's evidence indicates that:

(a) there is a substantial likelihood that final action by the court favorable to the petitioner would require of the respondent conduct or practices that would disrupt or be inconsistent with a regulatory scheme that regulates or covers the actions or transactions complained of by the petitioner established and administered under law by any state or federal regulatory board or officer acting under statutory authority of the commonwealth or of the United States; or

(b) that said regulatory board or officer has a substantial interest in reviewing said transactions or actions prior to judicial action under this chapter and that the said regulatory board or officer has the power to provide substantially the relief sought by the petitioner and the class, if any, which the petitioner represents, under this section.

Upon suspending proceedings under this section the court may enter any interlocutory or temporary orders it deems necessary and proper pending final action by the regulatory board or officer and trial, if any, in the court, including issuance of injunctions, certification of a class, and orders concerning the presentation of the matter to the regulatory board or officer. The court shall issue appropriate interlocutory orders, decrees and injunctions to preserve the status quo between the parties pending final action by the regulatory board or officer and trial and shall stay all proceedings in any court or before any regulatory board or officer in which petitioner and respondent are necessarily involved. The court may issue further orders, injunctions or other relief while the matter is before the regulatory board or officer and shall terminate the suspension and bring the matter forward for trial if it finds (a) that proceedings before the regulatory board or officer are unreasonably delayed or otherwise unreasonably prejudicial to the interests of a party before the court, or (b) that the regulatory board or officer has not taken final action within six months of the beginning of the order suspending proceedings under this chapter.

(8) Except as provided in section ten, recovering or failing to recover an award of damages or other relief in any administrative or judicial proceeding, except proceedings authorized by this section, by any person entitled to bring an action under this section, shall not constitute a bar to, or limitation upon relief authorized by this section.

Chapter 93A: Section 10. Notice to attorney general; injunction, prima facie evidence.

Section 10. Upon commencement of any action brought under section nine or section eleven, the clerk of the court shall mail a copy of the bill in equity to the attorney general and, upon entry of any judgment or decree in the action, the clerk of the court shall mail a copy of such judgment or decree to the attorney general.

Any permanent injunction or order of the court made under section four shall be prima facie evidence in an action brought under section nine or section eleven that the respondent used or employed an unfair or deceptive act or practice declared unlawful by section two.

Chapter 93A: Section 11. Persons engaged in business; actions for unfair trade practices; class actions; damages; injunction; costs.

Section 11. Any person who engages in the conduct of any trade or commerce and who suffers any loss of money or property, real or personal, as a result of the use or employment by another person who engages in any trade or commerce of an unfair method of competition or an unfair or deceptive act or practice declared unlawful by section two or by any rule or regulation issued under paragraph (c) of section two may, as hereinafter provided, bring an action in the superior court, or in the housing court as provided in section three of chapter one hundred and eighty-five C, whether by way of original complaint, counterclaim, cross-claim or third-party action for damages and such equitable relief, including an injunction, as the court deems to be necessary and proper.

Such person, if he has not suffered any loss of money or property, may obtain such an injunction if it can be shown that the aforementioned unfair method of competition, act or practice may have the effect of causing such loss of money or property.

Any persons entitled to bring such action may, if the use or employment of the unfair method of competition or the unfair or deceptive act or practice has caused similar injury to numerous other persons similarly situated and if the court finds in a preliminary hearing that he adequately and fairly represents such other persons, bring the action on behalf of himself and such other similarly injured and situated persons; the court shall require that notice of such action be given to unnamed petitioners in the most effective, practicable manner. Such action shall not be dismissed, settled or compromised without the approval of the court, and notice of any proposed dismissal, settlement or compromise shall be given to all members of the class of petitioners in such a manner as the court directs.

A person may assert a claim under this section in a district court, whether by way of original complaint, counterclaim, cross-claim or third-party action, for money damages only. Said damages may include double or treble damages, attorneys' fees and costs, as hereinafter provided, with provision for tendering by the person against whom the claim is asserted of a written offer of settlement for single damages, also as hereinafter provided. No rights to equitable relief shall be created under this paragraph, nor shall a person asserting such claim be able to assert any claim on behalf of other similarly injured and situated persons as provided in the preceding paragraph. The provisions of sections ninety-five to one hundred and ten, inclusive, of chapter two hundred and thirty-one, where applicable, shall apply to a claim under this section, except that the provisions for remand, removal and transfer shall be controlled by the amount of single damages claimed hereunder.

If the court finds for the petitioner, recovery shall be in the amount of actual damages; or up to three, but not less than two, times such amount if the court finds that the use or employment of the method of competition or the act or practice was a willful or knowing violation of said section two. For the purposes of this chapter, the amount of actual damages to be multiplied by the court shall be the amount of the judgment on all claims arising out of the same and underlying transaction or occurrence regardless of the existence or nonexistence of insurance coverage available in payment of the claim. In addition, the court shall award such other equitable relief, including an injunction, as it deems to be necessary and proper. The respondent may tender with his answer in any such action a written offer of settlement for single damages. If such tender or settlement is rejected by the petitioner, and if the court finds that the relief tendered was reasonable in relation to the injury actually suffered by the petitioner, then the court shall not award more than single damages.

If the court finds in any action commenced hereunder, that there has been a violation of section two, the petitioner shall, in addition to other relief provided for by this section and irrespective of the amount in controversy, be awarded reasonable attorneys' fees and costs incurred in said action.

In any action brought under this section, in addition to the provisions of paragraph (b) of section two, the court shall also be guided in its interpretation of unfair methods of competition by those provisions of chapter ninety-three known as the Massachusetts Antitrust Act.

No action shall be brought or maintained under this section unless the actions and transactions constituting the alleged unfair method of competition or the unfair or deceptive act or practice occurred primarily and substantially within the commonwealth. For the purposes of this paragraph, the burden of proof shall be upon the person claiming that such transactions and actions did not occur primarily and substantially within the commonwealth.

5. Sections 17200 to 17210 of the California Business and Professions Code

17200. As used in this chapter, unfair competition shall mean and include any unlawful, unfair or fraudulent business act or practice and unfair, deceptive, untrue or misleading advertising and any act prohibited by Chapter 1 (commencing with Section 17500) of Part 3 of Division 7 of the Business and Professions Code.

17201. As used in this chapter, the term person shall mean and include natural persons, corporations, firms, partnerships, joint stock companies, associations and other organizations of persons. 17201.5. As used in this chapter: (a) "Board within the Department of Consumer Affairs" includes any commission, bureau, division, or other similarly constituted agency within the Department of Consumer Affairs. (b) "Local consumer affairs agency" means and includes any city or county body which primarily provides consumer protection services.

17202. Notwithstanding Section 3369 of the Civil Code, specific or preventive relief may be granted to enforce a penalty, forfeiture, or penal law in a case of unfair competition.

17203. Any person who engages, has engaged, or proposes to engage in unfair competition may be enjoined in any court of competent jurisdiction. The court may make such orders or judgments, including the appointment of a receiver, as may be necessary to prevent the use or employment by any person of any practice which constitutes unfair competition, as defined in this chapter, or as may be necessary to restore to any person in interest any money or property, real or personal, which may have been acquired by means of such unfair competition.

17204. Actions for any relief pursuant to this chapter shall be prosecuted exclusively in a court of competent jurisdiction by the Attorney General or any district attorney or by any county counsel authorized by agreement with the district attorney in actions involving violation of a county ordinance, or any city attorney of a city, or city and county, having a population in excess of 750,000, and, with the consent of the district attorney, by a city prosecutor in any city having a full-time city prosecutor or, with the consent of the district attorney, by a city attorney in any city and county in the name of the people of the State of California upon their own complaint or upon the complaint of any board, officer, person, corporation or association or by any person acting for the interests of itself, its members or the general public.

17204.5. In addition to the persons authorized to bring an action pursuant to Section 17204, the City Attorney of the City of San Jose, with the annual consent of the Santa Clara County District Attorney, is authorized to prosecute those actions. This section shall remain in effect until such time as the population of the City of San Jose exceeds 750,000, as determined by the Population Research Unit of the Department of Finance, and at that time shall be repealed.

17205. Unless otherwise expressly provided, the remedies or penalties provided by this chapter are cumulative to each other and to the remedies or penalties available under all other laws of this state.

17206.

(a) Any person who engages, has engaged, or proposes to engage in unfair competition shall be liable for a civil penalty not to exceed two thousand five hundred dollars ($2,500) for each violation, which shall be assessed and recovered in a civil action brought in the name of the people of the State of California by the Attorney General, by any district attorney, by any county counsel authorized by agreement with the district attorney in actions involving violation of a county ordinance, by any city attorney of a city, or city and county, having a population in excess of 750,000, with the consent of the district attorney, by a city prosecutor in any city having a full-time city prosecutor, or, with the consent of the district attorney, by a city attorney in any city and county, in any court of competent jurisdiction.

(b) The court shall impose a civil penalty for each violation of this chapter. In assessing the amount of the civil penalty, the court shall consider any one or more of the relevant circumstances presented by any of the parties to the case, including, but not limited to, the following: the nature and seriousness of the misconduct, the number of violations, the persistence of the misconduct, the length of time over which the misconduct occurred, the willfulness of the defendant's misconduct, and the defendant's assets, liabilities, and net worth.

(c) If the action is brought by the Attorney General, one-half of the penalty collected shall be paid to the treasurer of the county in which the judgment was entered, and one-half to the State General Fund. If the action is brought by a district attorney or county counsel, the penalty collected shall be paid to the treasurer of the county in which the judgment was entered. Except as provided in subdivision(d), if the action is brought by a city attorney or city prosecutor, one-half of the penalty collected shall be paid to the treasurer of the city in which the judgment was entered, and one-half to the treasurer of the county in which the judgment was entered.

(d) If the action is brought at the request of a board within the Department of Consumer Affairs or a local consumer affairs agency, the court shall determine the reasonable expenses incurred by the board or local agency in the investigation and prosecution of the action. Before any penalty collected is paid out pursuant to subdivision (c), the amount of any reasonable expenses incurred by the board shall be paid to the state Treasurer for deposit in the special fund of the board described in Section 205. If the board has no such special fund, the moneys shall be paid to the state Treasurer. The amount of any reasonable expenses incurred by a local consumer affairs agency shall be paid to the general fund of the municipality or county that funds the local agency.

(e) If the action is brought by a city attorney of a city and county, the entire amount of the penalty collected shall be paid to the treasurer of the city and county in which the judgment was entered. However, if the action is brought by a city attorney of a city and county for the purposes of civil enforcement pursuant to Section 17980 of the Health and Safety Code or Article 3 (commencing with Section 11570) of Chapter 10 of Division 10 of the Health and Safety Code, either the penalty collected shall be paid entirely to the treasurer of the city and county in which the judgment was entered or, upon the request of the city attorney, the court may order that up to one-half of the penalty, under court supervision and approval, be paid for the purpose of restoring, maintaining, or enhancing the premises that were the subject of the action, and that the balance of the penalty be paid to the treasurer of the city and county.

17206.1.

(a) In addition to any liability for a civil penalty pursuant to Section 17206, any person who violates this chapter, and the act or acts of unfair competition are perpetrated against one or more senior citizens or disabled persons, may be liable for a civil penalty not to exceed two thousand five hundred dollars ($2,500) for each violation, which may be assessed and recovered in a civil action as prescribed in Section 17206. Subject to subdivision (d), any civil penalty shall be paid as prescribed by subdivisions (b) and (c) of Section 17206.

(b) As used in this section, the following terms have the following meanings: (1) "Senior citizen" means a person who is 65 years of age or older. (2) "Disabled person" means any person who has a physical or mental impairment which substantially limits one or more major life activities.

(A) As used in this subdivision, "physical or mental impairment" means any of the following: (i) Any physiological disorder or condition, cosmetic disfigurement, or anatomical loss substantially affecting one or more of the following body systems: neurological; muscoloskeletal; special sense organs; respiratory, including speech organs; cardiovascular;

reproductive; digestive; genitourinary; hemic and lymphatic; skin; or endocrine. (ii) Any mental or psychological disorder, such as mental retardation, organic brain syndrome, emotional or mental illness, and specific learning disabilities. The term "physical or mental impairment" includes, but is not limited to, such diseases and conditions as orthopedic, visual, speech and hearing impairment, cerebral palsy, epilepsy, muscular dystrophy, multiple sclerosis, cancer, heart disease, diabetes, mental retardation, and emotional illness.

(B) "Major life activities" means functions such as caring for one's self, performing manual tasks, walking, seeing, hearing, speaking, breathing, learning, and working.

(c) In determining whether to impose a civil penalty pursuant to subdivision (a) and the amount thereof, the court shall consider, in addition to any other appropriate factors, the extent to which one or more of the following factors are present: (1) Whether the defendant knew or should have known that his or her conduct was directed to one or more senior citizens or disabled persons. (2) Whether the defendant's conduct caused one or more senior citizens or disabled persons to suffer: loss or encumbrance of a primary residence, principal employment, or source of income; substantial loss of property set aside for retirement, or for personal or family care and maintenance; or substantial loss of payments received under a pension or retirement plan or a government benefits program, or assets essential to the health or welfare of the senior citizen or disabled person. (3) Whether one or more senior citizens or disabled persons are substantially more vulnerable than other members of the public to the defendant's conduct because of age, poor health or infirmity, impaired understanding, restricted mobility, or disability, and actually suffered substantial physical, emotional, or economic damage resulting from the defendant's conduct.

(d) Any court of competent jurisdiction hearing an action pursuant to this section may make orders and judgments as may be necessary to restore to any senior citizen or disabled person any money or property, real or personal, which may have been acquired by means of a violation of this chapter. Restitution ordered pursuant to this subdivision shall be given priority over recovery of any civil penalty designated by the court as imposed pursuant to subdivision (a), but shall not be given priority over any civil penalty imposed pursuant to subdivision (a) of Section 17206. If the court determines that full restitution cannot be made to those senior citizens or disabled persons, either at the time of judgment or by a future date determined by the court, then restitution under this subdivision shall be made on a pro rata basis depending on the amount of loss.

17206.5. In addition to the persons authorized to bring an action pursuant to Section 17206, the City Attorney of the City of San Jose, with the annual consent of the Santa Clara County District Attorney, is authorized to prosecute those actions. This section shall remain in effect until such time as the population of the City of San Jose exceeds 750,000, as determined by the Population Research Unit of the Department of Finance, and at that time shall be repealed.

17207.

(a) Any person who intentionally violates any injunction prohibiting unfair competition issued pursuant to Section 17203 shall be liable for a civil penalty not to exceed six thousand dollars ($6,000) for each violation. Where the conduct constituting a violation is of a continuing nature, each day of that conduct is a separate and distinct violation. In determining the amount of the civil penalty, the court shall consider all relevant circumstances, including, but not limited to, the extent of the harm caused by the conduct constituting a violation, the nature and persistence of that conduct, the length of time over which the conduct occurred, the assets, liabilities, and net worth of the person, whether corporate or individual, and any corrective action taken by the defendant.

(b) The civil penalty prescribed by this section shall be assessed and recovered in a civil action brought in any county in which the violation occurs or where the injunction was issued in the name of the people of the State of California by the Attorney General or by any district attorney, any county counsel authorized by agreement with the district attorney in actions involving violation of a county ordinance, or any city attorney in any court of competent jurisdiction within his or her jurisdiction without regard to the county from which the original injunction was issued. An action brought pursuant to this section to recover civil penalties shall take precedence over all civil matters on the calendar of the court except those matters to which equal precedence on the calendar is granted by law.

(c) If such an action is brought by the Attorney General, one-half of the penalty collected pursuant to this section shall be paid to the treasurer of the county in which the judgment was entered, and one-half to the State Treasurer. If brought by a district attorney or county counsel the entire amount of the penalty collected shall be paid to the treasurer of the county in which the judgment is entered. If brought by a city attorney or city prosecutor, one-half of the penalty shall be paid to the treasurer of the county in which the judgment was entered and one-half to the city, except that if the action was brought by a city attorney of a city and county the entire amount of the penalty collected shall be paid to the treasurer of the city and county in which the judgment is entered.

(d) If the action is brought at the request of a board within the Department of Consumer Affairs or a local consumer affairs agency, the court shall determine the reasonable expenses incurred by the board or local agency in the investigation and prosecution of the action. Before any penalty collected is paid out pursuant to subdivision (c), the amount of the reasonable expenses incurred by the board shall be paid to the State Treasurer for deposit in the special fund of the board described in Section 205. If the board has no such special fund, the moneys shall be paid to the State Treasurer. The amount of the reasonable expenses incurred by a local consumer affairs agency shall be paid to the general fund of the municipality or county which funds the local agency.

17208. Any action to enforce any cause of action pursuant to this chapter shall be commenced within four years after the cause of action accrued. No cause of action barred under existing law on the effective date of this section shall be revived by its enactment.

17209. If a violation of this chapter is alleged or the application or construction of this chapter is in issue in any proceeding in the Supreme Court of California, a state court of appeal, or the appellate division of a superior court, the person who commenced that proceeding shall serve notice thereof, including a copy of the person's brief or petition and brief, on the Attorney General, directed to the attention of the Consumer Law Section, and on the district attorney of the county in which the lower court action or proceeding was originally filed. The notice, including the brief or petition and brief, shall be served within three days after the commencement of the appellate proceeding, provided that the time may be extended by the Chief Justice or presiding justice or judge for good cause shown. No judgment or relief, temporary or permanent, shall be granted until proof of service of this notice is filed with the court.

17210.

(a) For purposes of this section, "hotel" means any hotel, motel, bed and breakfast inn, or other similar transient lodging establishment, but it does not include any residential hotel as defined in Section 50519 of the Health and Safety Code. "Innkeeper" means the owner or operator of a hotel, or the duly authorized agent or employee of the owner or operator.

(b) For purposes of this section, "handbill" means, and is specifically limited to, any tangible commercial solicitation to guests of the hotel urging that they patronize any commercial enterprise.

(c) Every person (hereinafter "distributor") engages in unfair competition for purposes of this chapter who deposits, places, throws, scatters, casts, or otherwise distributes any handbill to any individual guest rooms in any hotel, including, but not limited to, placing, throwing, leaving, or attaching any handbill adjacent to, upon, or underneath any guest room door, doorknob, or guest room entryway, where either the innkeeper has expressed objection to handbill distribution, either orally to the distributor or by the posting of a sign or other notice in a conspicuous place within the lobby area and at all points of access from the exterior of the premises to guest room areas indicating that handbill distribution is prohibited, or the distributor has received written notice pursuant to subdivision (e) that the innkeeper has expressed objection to the distribution of handbills to guest rooms in the hotel.

(d) Every person (hereinafter "contractor") engages in unfair competition for purposes of this chapter who causes or directs any other person, firm, business, or entity to distribute, or cause the distribution of, any handbill to any individual guest rooms in any hotel in violation of subdivision (c) of this section, if the contractor has received written notice from the innkeeper objecting to the distribution of handbills to individual guest rooms in the hotel.

(e) Every contractor who causes or directs any distributor to distribute, or cause the distribution of, any handbills to any individual guest rooms in any hotel, if the contractor has received written notice from the innkeeper or from any other contractor or intermediary pursuant to this subdivision, objecting to the distribution of handbills to individual guest rooms in the hotel has failed to provide a written copy of that notice to each distributor prior to the commencement of distribution of handbills by the distributor or by any person hired or retained by the distributor for that purpose, or, within 24 hours following the receipt of the notice by the contractor if received after the commencement of distribution, and has failed to instruct and demand any distributor to not distribute, or to cease the distribution of, the handbills to individual guest rooms in any hotel for which such a notice has been received is in violation of this section.

(f) Any written notice given, or caused to be given, by the innkeeper pursuant to or required by any provision of this section shall be deemed to be in full force and effect until such time as the notice is revoked in writing.

(g) Nothing in this section shall be deemed to prohibit the distribution of a handbill to guest rooms in any hotel where the distribution has been requested or approved in writing by the innkeeper, or to any individual guest room when the occupant thereof has affirmatively requested or approved the distribution of the handbill during the duration of the guest's occupancy.

LIST OF STATE LITTLE FTC ACTS, UDAP, AND GENERAL CONSUMER PROTECTION STATUTES

A survey of the substantive provisions of the various state laws governing false advertising, unfair and deceptive acts and practices, and other general consumer protection issues is well beyond the scope of this handbook.   However, below is a list of state statutes fitting this description at the time of writing.   Counsel faced with the prospect of pursuing or defending a consumer protection claim under unfamiliar state law may find it useful to start with the appropriate statutory sections and research the annotations provided in most published compilations of state law, or conduct computerized research on these citations using online legal research tools. This list does *not* include consumer-oriented statutes pertaining to specific product categories or areas of commerce, which may be relevant to the particular claim of interest.

- Deceptive Trade Practices Act, ALA. CODE. §§ 8-19-1 *et seq.* (2003)
- Consumer Protection Act, ALASKA STAT. §§ 45.50.471 to 45.50.561 (Michie 2002)
- Consumer Fraud Act, ARIZ. REV. STAT. §§ 44-1521 *et seq.* (2003)
- Deceptive Trade Practices Act, ARK. CODE §§ 4-88-101 *et seq.* (2003)
- Consumers Legal Remedies Act, CAL. CIV. CODE §§ 1750 to 1784 (West 2003)
- CAL. BUS. & PROF. CODE §§ 17200 *et seq.*, 17500 *et seq.* (West 2003)
- Colorado Consumer Protection Act, COLO. REV. STAT. §§ 6-1-101 *et seq.* (2003)
- Connecticut Unfair Trade Practices Act, CONN. GEN. STAT. §§ 42-110a *et seq.* (2003)
- Consumer Fraud Act, DEL. CODE tit. 6, §§ 2511 *et seq.* (2003)
- Uniform Deceptive Trade Practices Act, DEL. CODE tit. 6, §§ 2531 *et seq.* (2003)
- District of Columbia Consumer Protection Procedures Act, D.C. CODE §§ 28-3901 to 28-3909 (2003)
- Deceptive and Unfair Trade Practices Act, FLA. STAT. ch. 501.201 *et seq.* (2003)

- Fair Business Practices Act of 1975, GA. CODE §§ 10-1-370 *et seq.* (2003)
- HAW. REV. STAT. § 480-2 (2003)
- Uniform Deceptive Trade Practice Act, HAW. REV. STAT. §§ 481A *et seq.* (2003)
- Consumer Protection Act, IDAHO CODE §§ 48-601 *et seq.* (Michie 2003)
- Consumer Fraud and Deceptive Business Practices Act, 815 ILL. COMP. STAT. 505/1 *et seq.* (2003)
- Uniform Deceptive Trade Practices Act, 815 ILL. COMP. STAT. 510/1 *et seq.* (2003)
- Deceptive Consumer Sales Act, IND. CODE §§ 24-5-0.5-1 *et seq.* (2003)
- Iowa Consumer Fraud Act, IOWA CODE § 714.16 (2003)
- Consumer Protection Act, KAN. STAT. §§ 50-623 *et seq.* (2002)
- Consumer Protection Act, KY. REV. STAT. §§ 367.110 to 367.300 (Michie 2003)
- Unfair Trade Practices and Consumer Protection Law, LA. REV. STAT. §§ 51:1401 *et seq.* (West 2002)
- Maine Unfair Trade Practices Act, ME. REV. STAT. tit. 5, §§ 205-A *et seq.* (West 2003)
- Uniform Deceptive Trade Practices Act, ME. REV. STAT. tit. 10, §§ 1211 to 1216 (2003)
- Consumer Protection Act, MD. CODE ANN., COM. LAW I §§ 13-101 *et seq.*, 14-101 (2003)
- Consumer Protection Act, MASS. GEN. LAWS ch. 93A (2003)
- Michigan Consumer Protection Act, MICH. COMP. LAWS § 445.901 (2003)
- MINN. STAT. § 8.31 (2003)
- Unlawful Trade Practices Act, MINN. STAT. § 325D.09 to 325D.16 (2003)
- Deceptive Trade Practices Act, MINN. STAT. § 325D.44 to 325D.48 (2003)
- False Advertising Act, MINN. STAT. § 325F.67 (2003)
- Consumer Fraud Act, MINN. STAT. §§ 325F.68 to 325F.70 (2003)
- Consumer Protection Act, MISS. CODE ANN. §§ 75-24-1 *et seq.* (2003)
- Merchandising Purchases Act, MO. REV. STAT. §§ 407.010 *et seq.* (2003)
- Montana Consumer Protection Act, MONT. CODE §§ 30-14-101 *et seq.* (2003)

- Consumer Protection Act, NEB. REV. STAT. §§ 59-1601 *et seq.* (2003)
- Uniform Deceptive Trade Practices Act, NEB. REV. STAT. §§ 87-302 *et seq.* (2003)
- Deceptive Trade Practices Act, NEV. REV. STAT. §§ 598.0903 *et seq.* (2002)
- NEV. REV. STAT. §§ 41.600 *et seq.* (2002)
- New Hampshire Consumer Protection Act, N.H. REV. STAT. ANN. § 358-A (2003)
- Consumer Fraud Act, N.J. STAT. ANN. §§ 56:8-1 *et seq.* (West 2003)
- Unfair Trade Practices Act, N.M. STAT. ANN. §§ 57-12-1 *et seq.* (Michie 2003)
- N.Y. EXEC. LAW § 63(12) (McKinney 2003)
- N.Y. GEN. BUS. LAW §§ 349, 350 (McKinney 2003.)
- Unfair and Deceptive Trade Practices Act, N.C. GEN. STAT. §§ 75-1.1 *et seq.* (2003)
- Consumer Fraud and Unlawful Credit Practices, N.D. CENT. CODE §§ 51-15-01 *et seq.* (2003)
- Consumer Sales Practice Act, OHIO REV. CODE §§ 1345.01 *et seq.* (West 2003)
- OHIO REV. CODE § 4165 (West 2003)
- Consumer Protection Act, OKLA. STAT. tit. 15, §§ 751 *et seq.* (West 2003)
- Oklahoma Deceptive Trade Practices Act, OKLA. STAT. tit. 78, §§ 51 *et seq.* (West 2003)
- Unlawful Trade Practices Act, OR. REV. STAT. §§ 646.605 *et seq.* (2001)
- Unfair Trade Practices and Consumer Protection Law, PA. STAT. ANN. tit. 73, §§ 201 *et seq.* (West 2003)
- Unfair Trade Practice and Consumer Protection Act, R.I. GEN. LAWS §§ 6-13.1-1 *et seq.* (2002)
- Unfair Trade Practices Act, S.C. CODE ANN. §§ 39-5-10 *et seq.* (Law Co-op 2003)
- South Dakota Deceptive Trade Practices and Consumer Protection Law, S.D. CODIFIED LAWS §§ 37-24-1 to 37-24-35 *et seq.* (Michie 2003)
- Consumer Protection Act, TENN. CODE ANN. §§ 47-18-101 *et seq.* (2003)
- Deceptive Trade Practices and Consumer Protection Act, TEX. BUS. & COM. CODE §§ 17.41 *et seq.* (Vernon 2003)
- Unfair Practices Act, UTAH CODE § 13-5 (2003)

- Utah Consumer Sales Practices Act, UTAH CODE § 13-11 (2003)
- Consumer Fraud Act, VT. STAT. ANN. tit. 9, §§ 2451 *et seq.* (2003)
- Virginia Consumer Protection Act, VA. CODE §§ 59.1-196 *et seq.* (Michie 2003)
- Virginia Prizes and Gifts Act, VA. CODE §§ 59.1-415 *et seq.* (Michie 2003)
- Unfair Business Practices/Consumer Protection Act, WASH. REV. CODE § 19.86 (2003)
- West Virginia Consumer Credit and Protection Act, W. VA. CODE §§ 46A-6-101 *et seq.* (2003)
- Wisconsin Law Prohibiting Fraudulent Advertising, WIS. STAT. § 100.18 (2003)
- WIS. STAT. § 100.20 (2003)
- Wyoming Consumer Protection Act, WYO. STAT. §§ 40-12-101 *et seq.* (Michie 2002)

TABLE OF CASES

A

B

C

D

E

F

G

K

L

M

N

O

S

T

U

V

W

Y

Z

ABA SECTION OF ANTITRUST LAW
COMMITMENT TO QUALITY

The Section of Antitrust Law is committed to the highest standards of scholarship and continuing legal education. To that end, each of our books and treatises is subjected to rigorous quality control mechanisms throughout the design, drafting, editing, and peer review processes. Each Section publication is drafted and edited by leading experts on the topics covered and then rigorously peer reviewed by the Section's Books and Treatises Committee, at least two Council members, and then other officers and experts. Because the Section's quality commitment does not stop at publication, we encourage you to provide any comments or suggestions you may have for future editions of this book or other publications.

Defending Liberty
Pursuing Justice